FOR

LAND SAKES

73 YEARS

IN

REAL ESTATE

NORTHERN INDIANA
HISTORICAL SOCIETY

J. W. Fieldhouse meat delivery wagon in front of market he ran from 1873 to 1883. The room above drug store was where Charles G. Conn first started making mouth pieces and band instruments. Made his first cornet in 1875.

FOR

LAND SAKES

73 Years
In Real Estate

By CHARLES H. FIELDHOUSE

SERVICE PRESS — PRINTERS
ELKHART, INDIANA
JUNE, 1957

NORTHERN INDIANA
HISTORICAL SOCIETY

PRINTED IN THE UNITED STATES OF AMERICA

M OST of this book is about diffierent things that happened during a period of seventy three years, from 1883 to 1956, in one office location at 111 W. Lexington Avenue, Elkhart, Indiana.

This office has been occupied by John W. Fieldhouse from 1883 to 1938, 55 years, and by his son, Charles H. Fieldhouse, from June 1, 1901 to June 1, 1956, each carrying the keys to the office for more than 55 years, from the horse and buggy days to the automobile days.

John W. Fieldhouse was born October 15, 1850 on a 90 acre farm two miles south of White Pigeon, Michigan. His father came to America from Acomb, York, England in 1832, when he was 20 years old. He came in a sailing vessel which took 6 weeks to cross the Atlantic. He was seasick most of the trip, so never went back to see his folks and seven brothers and sisters.

From New York City he came by boat up the Hudson River, through the Erie Canal to Buffalo, on Lake Erie to Toledo and from there by stage to White Pigeon, where he knew someone from his home town, who had located there.

Later on he married Hannah Barker, who had also come from Acomb, York, England. They did not know each other until they met in White Pigeon.

They bought a 90 acre farm south of White Pigeon for $2.50 an acre and had a family of seven children, four boys and three girls. John W. Fieldhouse was the last child to arrive. When the 4 boys were young their father set aside ten acres for them to use, and whatever they raised, they could count as their own. John remained on the farm until he was 20 years old.

His brother Edward, who was 4 years older, had saved $1,300.00 by 1868. In that spring he bought 1,300 sheep. During the Civil War the boys had planted their ten acres to wheat, which brought $3.00 per bushel at harvest time. The boys knew how hard they had worked for the money they saved, and were encouraged by their father. On account of the farm being small, only 90 acres, John Fieldhouse also went to adjoining farms with his brothers and sheared sheep in the spring of each year at ten cents a head, also helped the neighbors plant corn at 25 cents a day plus a good noon meal. In this way the boys all had some money of their own.

Edward with his 1,300 sheep started for Chicago or what is now known as South Chicago, and all four brothers helped to drive them through, as reports were that there was plenty of pasture in that locality. It took ten days to make the trip, as the sheep had to walk every foot of the way, a distance of about 125 miles, and the roads were very dusty. The sheep would eat along the side of the road as they went and the only conveyance was what was known then as a democrat wagon, one seat, no top, but a rather long light wagon box behind, drawn by one horse. In this wagon were iron rods and three foot wide canvas, enough to enclose these 1,300 sheep at night, and a small tent which housed the 5 men who drove the flock.

The first night was spent just off the Bristol and Elkhart Road about one mile east of Elkhart's limits. The next morning the sheep were driven through Elkhart, after they had pastured several hours and were driven to the St. Joseph River for water. It was some sight for the town's people to see this large flock of sheep go through Elkhart and many people remembered and often mentioned it years later. It was rather hard work driving them, as sheep usually want to turn back, or go the wrong way. They had one shepherd dog, well trained to assist them.

The men got their own breakfast, but dinner and supper were usually bought at farm houses along the way at a very small price, compared to prices of today. After 4 nights, near LaPorte the sheep were counted for the first time and it was discovered that 46 were missing. It was later found that all 46 sheep were bought from one farmer, as each separate flock usually mingle together. Edward Fieldhouse, owner of all the sheep, started back alone in the wagon to find them. He inquired along the way if anyone had seen any wandering sheep. At the west edge of Bristol he was rejoiced to find that farmer Palen had seen the big flock go past and a few days later discovered the 46 sheep wandering back toward their former home. He knew there would be someone along looking for them later, so he turned them into a field of weeds he had. Arrangements were made to leave them on the Palen farm for the balance of the summer, after which Edward Fieldhouse drove back west of LaPorte, where he found the balance of the large flock had been driven slowly about ten miles nearer the free summer pasture lands where they were going. After arriving at the low marsh lands of what is now South Chicago, Edward Fieldhouse, a hired man and the shepherd dog remained there nearly three months, living in a tent, watching the sheep and keeping them watered and fed.

It was rather lonesome work, but the sheep were growing heavier on the heavy grass which grew there. One day as the two men were watching the sheep together at the edge of a growth of brush, they were startled by a noise behind them and as they rose to their feet a hunter remarked to them, "You got up just in time, I was ready to shoot, as I thought it was a fox I was after". It was a very close call for one of them as the moving of the brush was almost a sure sign for the hunter that it was the fox, which he had seen just a few minutes before go in that same direction. Many a life has since been lost that same way.

In the fall the sheep were driven to the Chicago Stock Yards and sold at a good profit for Edward Fieldhouse. In a few days he came with John to the Palen farm and drove the 46 sheep to Elkhart, where they tried to sell the flock, but were unsuccessful, so they drove them to James R. Mather's farm, just in the rear or south of where Vistula and Franklin Streets meet today. This J. R. Mather had recently given a part of his farm to the Lake Shore & Michigan Southern Railway, now known as New York Central Railway, on the promise that they would build railway repair shops on the property. These shops had just been finished a short time before.

The two stayed at the Mather farm over night. The next morning they killed and butchered six of the sheep, placed the meat in the democrat wagon and started out from house to house to sell it. They did not stop until they had sold all of the 46 sheep. This surprised Edward Fieldhouse so much that he decided to start a meat market in Elkhart, but could not find a suitable building, as the shops having been built, all of the store buildings were filled.

Within ten days he bought a lot at what is now 121 West Jackson Boulevard and William Barger, a local contractor, built him a two story building 18 by 75 feet with basement complete for $1,500.00. Within a short time Edward Fieldhouse's meat market was a reality. Shortly afterward, Edward Fieldhouse married the daughter of James R. Mather and they lived above the market the balance of his lifetime.

About 1870, John W. Fieldhouse decided to join with him in partnership with $500.00 he had saved. The two worked together early and late, opening the market at 5 A.M., closing each evening at 8:30 P.M. During this period, each night John slept in the rear room of the market and got his meals at the Elkhart House, a hotel which stood a little west of the market. The hotel was a good customer of the market, as well as the Clifton House, now known as Hotel Bucklen. They also had the Depot Hotel.

They aimed to carry the best of meat and it was difficult in those days to keep a full stock, as all meat sold was locally butchered. They also established their own slaughter house, which greatly helped to keep a full meat supply. It was John's job to go out through the country with team and wagon and buy stock, bring it in or arrange with local boys to drive stock and sheep in on foot.

Trips were made in all directions, but most of the buying was north of Elkhart as far as twenty miles. This work was an education to John as sometimes he made poor buys, other times good. There were many tricks in this kind of dealing, but he soon learned the weight of an animal just by looking at it and often bought by guess when there were no scales handy.

He well remembered the old circus man P. T. Barnum, who a number of times personally called at the Fieldhouse market to buy meat for the circus. Barnum always bought nothing but the best quality and picked out the meat himself. Once the market boy, Mike Whitmeyer, who helped in the market many years, asked Barnum for a ticket to the show. Barnum said, "You want me to give you a ticket?" Mike said "Yes". Barnum said, "Can you give me that calf?" Mike shook his head no, but as Barnum left he said to Mike, "Come down this evening and I will be there to let you in." Mike saw the show and told everyone years later that he knew P. T. Barnum.

One time Ringling Brothers' one ring circus came to Elkhart and put up their tent west of the Pigeon Street bridge, (now Lexington Ave.). At that time they only had one elephant and the keeper of the elephant, noticing the St. Joseph River flowed past the circus grounds, decided to give the elephant a bath. Taking the elephant out in three feet of water, he tried to get the elephant to lie down in the water, but was unsuccessful. The elephant placed its trunk around the keeper's body and held him under water until he was drowned. That afternoon and evening the elephant performed in the one ring circus just the same as usual, for the circus people all knew that the elephant was justified in killing the keeper, as two weeks before the elephant had been chained to a tree and horsewhipped by the keeper. The elephant appeared natural there-after, but it did not forget.

On July 3, 1873, in the morning, the icemen came in the back door of the meat market to fill the top of the large ice refrigerator. They mentioned there was a circus in LaPorte, forty miles from Elkhart. They were going to try to make the train to see the show there that afternoon and on account of being in a hurry they were going to put the 200 pound ice cakes in without cutting them in two. They asked for help, so Edward Fieldhouse consented and as they pulled the first cake up the slanting plank, a sharp sound came from the icebox, but no one thought much of it and several cakes were put in, but when the third one was almost in, the pulley broke and it caused Edward to fall to the floor with his head next to the wall at the end of the plank. At the next second the 200 pound cake of ice went heavily against his head, causing him to die within one hour, leaving his wife a widow with a son about two years old. John was at the meat counter and helped carry his brother to the home above the market. It was a sad Fourth of July that year for John Field-house. His father and mother wanted him to come back to the farm, but John liked the market better than the farm, so he continued with the business until 1883.

Frank Timmis appeared one day, a former neighbor boy who had just returned from a three year stay at the diamond fields of South

Fieldhouse office in 1902.

Africa, where he had worked with an uncle for three years digging for diamonds. During that period he had made $25,000.00, and had brought it all back with him. He would have stayed longer but was afraid to, as there were many fights and holdups around the diamond mines at that period. He noticed that John Fieldhouse was very busy and doing a good business, which he seemed to like. He offered to buy everything at invoice. The deal was made, after a few weeks training. John Fieldhouse started out to collect some back bills he had outstanding. John was a married man now and owned his home at 209 South Second Street, which he had built before he married Mary J. Hubbard, a farm girl, who lived with her parents on a 154 acre farm 4 miles southwest of Elkhart. After several weeks' time trying to collect some old outstanding bills, John decided he could make money easier in other ways than trying to collect old accounts. Everyone seemed to be hard up, so he just forgot about his book accounts and looked around for a better way to make money. After loafing several months he estimated his total worth at $30,000.00, which he had made in about ten years' time in the meat market. So he bought a frame building at 111 W. Pigeon Street, (now Lexington Ave.), from a man named Mike Truby, who operated a book and jewelry store in the room. He also bought, at the same time, a frame store building on the next lot east and a frame dwelling adjoining on the west. In addition to the above property, he had formerly built a one story house on Cone Street, which he rented as a side line while operating the market.

While Mr. Truby was moving from the building, John was walking around Elkhart and he finally decided to open a real estate office in the Truby room, as the store on the east was occupied as a small grocery and the house was occupied as a residence. A four room apartment was above the Truby room.

In front of the Truby store the first cement sidewalk was laid in the City of Elkhart, prior to the purchase of the property by John. Board or wooden sidewalks were popular before that date, and plank crossings were used at many street intersections. Oil lamps and gas lamps were used as street lights and the lamp lighter came with a small ladder each evening and morning to turn them on and off. In 1883 there were no electric lights in the City of Elkhart, although Elkhart was the first city in the state to have electric operated street cars, which came in about 1890. Just before this period the first electric lights came in and the first one was displayed in the Frank Sell Jewelry Store window at 311 South Main Street. At first breakdowns were numerous and such stores and residences that used them had combination fixtures, which were both gas and electric, so when the electricity failed, gas lights could be turned on.

John bought the Truby desk and safe and with three chairs and a wood burning stove, his real estate office was open for business. The front room of his office was 11 feet wide and 24 feet deep, the back room was 16 feet square. This frame building he used until 1903, when he had the building moved to an adjoining lot to the west, while a new brick building was built on about the same plan as the old frame building. After we moved into the new office, the old one was torn down.

During John Fieldhouse's real estate career of 55 years, his residence was less than one block from the office, being located at 209 South Second Street up to the year 1892, in which year he built a new home at 201 South Second Street, at the southwest corner of Pigeon Street (now Lexington Ave.) where Alma, my wife and I are living today. At the time we moved into the new house our family, in addition to mother and father, were my two sisters and myself. One sister still resides in Elkhart and the other one has lived in Bradenton, Florida for many years. During each year many people, knowing that Alma and I occupy this house, ask this question: "How many rooms are there in your home?" My reply always is: "Counting the attic and basement, there are 21 rooms." Their next question usually is: "Does Alma look after the cleaning of all those rooms?" To which my reply always is: "That is in the contract."

To show how things change, when this house was built in 1892, there were five city blocks on Second Street between our house and the railroad depot, with many homes in each block. Today in 1956, Dr. Milo Lundt, Helen Lundt and their son, plus Alma and I are the only people living in dwelling houses in the entire five city blocks. The old landmarks are fast disappearing, showing that it is a changing world.

My father's first real estate business was three acres of ground, less than five blocks from his office, which he platted and named a new street Pacific Street, with lots on both sides numbered from 1 to 20. He called this new addition, after having it surveyed, staked out and recorded in the Courthouse in Goshen, Fieldhouse's First Addition to the City of Elkhart. However, the lots did not seem to sell, so he built a house on one of them, hiring a mason and carpenter. When completed there was a basement, 5 rooms down and 2 upstairs and he offered it for sale at $1,000.00 cash including the lot. For the following three months it stood vacant with a "For Sale" sign on it, which made John feel very much discouraged.

Today it seems strange that one could build a 7 room dwelling and include the lot at a selling price of $1,000.00, unless one stole the lumber. But times have changed since 1884, as our old books, which we have had in the

cupboard at the office for the past 73 years
of real estate business, show that all the lumber cost, including roof shingles was $140.00
for a 7 room house. Common labor one could
hire at 10 cents per hour, $1.00 per day, $6.00
per week at 10 hours per day. Carpenters 12½
cents per hour, $1.25 per day, $7.50 per week.
Masons 15 cents per hour, $1.50 per day, $9.00
per week. Man with team, dirt wagon and self
$2.00 per day, $12.00 per week. As a last effort, John placed an advertisement in the Elkhart Daily Review: "Seven room, new house
for sale on Pacific Street with lot for $1,000.00,
$100.00 down and balance $10.00 per month,
plus 6% interest, payable monthly." He immediately had three buyers for the house. It
was sold on monthly contract and John immediately built two more houses for the other
two customers, for he had found a new way to
sell real estate.

At a real estate convention at Indianapolis
many years later, in telling of this experience,
it was mentioned that he may have been the
first man in the State of Indiana, who sold
real estate on the monthly installment plan.
Using his plan John was able to sell houses as
fast as he could build them. He was active as a
builder from 1884 to 1931, in which year he
stopped, due to the depression. It was well
he did, for in the following year 1932, his office had 38 vacant houses and some of them
stood vacant for as long as three years. The
office also had five store rooms vacant and

this fact discouraged him from any further building. He however, during this fifty year period, laid out the following additions:

Fieldhouse's 1st Add., consisting of	20 lots
Fieldhouse's 2nd Add., consisting of	53 lots
Fieldhouse's 3rd Add., consisting of	63 lots
Fieldhouse's 4th Add., consisting of	70 lots
Fieldhouse's 5th Add., consisting of	23 lots
Fieldhouse's 6th Add., consisting of	14 lots
Fieldhouse's 7th Add., consisting of	14 lots
Fieldhouse's 8th Add., consisting of	27 lots
Fieldhouse's 9th Add., consisting of	9 lots
Fieldhouse's 10th Add., consisting of	15 lots
Fieldhouse's East Side Addition	29 lots
Fieldhouse's West Side Addition	343 lots
Extension of Fieldhouse's East Side	29 lots
Sub-Division of Part of Outlot 23	34 lots

Total No. of lots platted in 50 years 743

Most of these additions he built up as he laid them out. He would first have them leveled and graded by hauling dirt with teams and wagons, filling low places. In his Fourth Addition, he hauled a total of 22,000 wagon loads of dirt from every dirt bank he could get dirt out of. Each summer when the St. Joseph River would get low, his crew of about 7 men, with scrapers, wagons and teams would haul all they could secure from the bed of the river. At one time he changed the course at the mouth of Christiana Creek, by making a new channel for it for a distance of about 300 feet and the depth they dug was as much as 20 feet.

At that time wagon boxes were mostly made of 2 by 4 inch lumber and the sideboards and bottom were taken apart in dumping each load, after which they were replaced by using a man at each end, and the box was ready for the next load to be shoveled in again by 3 or 4 men. It was a slow way compared to hauling dirt with power machinery as used today. But in those days all loads were drawn by horses up to the year 1915, with work days of ten hours and a six day week. But the good times went and came then, just the same as now, but it did not cost as much to live then as now.

In 1888 John sold lots on West Jefferson Street with a new seven room house on it, with furnace and bath, for a total price of $1,250.00. These houses are still standing today and have since sold as high at $7,000.00, although there have been some changes. In 1888 tin bath tubs were installed, which did not last, except in a few instances where these tin tubs were still in use after fifty years, but tin was a much better grade then, than it is now.

In 1892 business slowed down as hard times came on. One day a teamster came in the office and remarked to John that he was going to kill his team, as it was the month of January and he was out of hay and he mentioned another teamster who was going to do the same. John told him that he would have work for both teams in the spring and offered to loan both men money to buy feed, to which the men replied: "If you will buy us dynamite we will open the dirt bank and we will then keep wood fires burning during the night, so the bank will not freeze again." This was done, and dirt was hauled by five teams the balance of that winter, which was an extra cold one. Men and their teams of horses went through hardships in those days, but they got by and seemed to make the best of it. They enjoyed life and worked hard, ten hours a day during the summer, six days a week and called at the office each Saturday evening for their wages, as the office was open in those days from 7:30 A.M. to 8:30 P.M. closing one hour for dinner from 11:30 to 12:30 and one hour for supper from 5:30 to 6:30.

Before I came in the office John had no office help, but he would leave a note on his desk stating the time he would return. One day he came in and saw another note on the same sheet of paper, which read: "damn liar." The office was unlocked all day long.

John never worked on Sundays. When he was running the meat market, he worked one Sunday morning getting some hams ready to sell. He told the man he was selling them to, that they would be on the basement steps covered by a trap door in front of the market. There were $200.00 worth of these hams placed there Sunday evening, just before John went to bed. The man came for the hams at 4 A.M. There were no hams, for someone had stolen all of them.

One day John sold two of the South Bend Studebaker Brothers some land in Elkhart on the Elkhart River, which is now called Studebaker Park. John took ten Studebaker wagons in on the deal. He lined these ten wagons up in front of his place of business with a "For Sale" sign on them at a rather low price and within ten days they were all sold.

During the time when everyone worked ten hours a day, the Bucklen Theatre only averaged a road show about once every two weeks the year around, unless it was a stock company, which would stay a week and play a different show every night. There never was a year went past without having "Uncle Tom's Cabin," which would always have a full house of about 800 seats. Minstrel shows would appear several times a year and occasionally home talent shows. Today there are no Uncle Tom's Cabin or minstrel shows on the road, as moving pictures and higher railroad rates drove them off the road. At that time the Bucklen Opera House had no electric lights, but they had gas lights throughout the theatre, which could be turned up and down by several levers behind the scenes on the stage.

The good old days of 1893.

About 1895 the first moving picture was shown for only 5 minutes at the Bucklen Theatre, a scene at Atlantic City beach. The pictures at that time were poor, the films not perfected yet. There were black spots, thousands of them, but the idea was there, as one could see the waves and the swimmers. My father and mother and I used to attend all the shows, as my father was agent for H. E. Bucklen and it did not cost him anything to go. A man who hauled coal was in the office one night and remarked "John Fieldhouse, you are going to ruin your boy by taking him to all these road shows at the Bucklen Theatre." There was a man I was really mad at, but it turned out all right, as my father afterwards took me to nearly every show just the same, as we all enjoyed going. When Dave Carpenter was running the theatre, lecture course tickets were sold each year for about ten lectures a season and people would stand in line several hours early in the morning for the 9 o'clock sale in order to reserve good seats. Famous speakers often came and these lectures were well attended, for there were no automobiles or movies in those days and many people enjoyed listening to the lectures. Sometimes there were lantern slide pictures and season tickets sold at low prices.

One time a sleight-of-hand performer visited the Bucklen Theatre for one night with full equipment weighing about 8 tons. He placed a young woman sitting on a trapeze bar ten feet above the stage with her hands on both ropes. He then stood in the audience and shot off a 45 caliber blank cartridge towards her. Upon hearing the loud report, she instantly vanished from sight right before the audience; the empty trapeze bar was left swinging. It was the most bewildering and perfect stage act ever seen by an Elkhart audience, as no one could understand where she went in a fraction of a second. The same man placed another woman in a box near the front of the stage. Ten minutes later the box was opened and she was not there. It evidently took heavy equipment to produce this act.

There was also the famous sawmill scene where the villian was tied to a 2½ foot thick log, his body traveling nearer and nearer the large spinning saw and when his body was about one inch from the saw the curtain came down. That was the way they did it in the early days of the Bucklen Theatre. The pony express man rode his horse on a treadmill and it was a good act. Sometimes there was what looked like a real train going across the back part of the stage and the drunkard's wife turned the switch just one second before the train passed.

One time an actor was called out on the stage several times by hand clapping. He finally stepped to the front lights and made a short talk, something like this: "Elkhart citizens, I want to make a few remarks about your theatre orchestra. We have traveled in many cities throughout the United States, but your Elkhart orchestra is about the best we have ever encountered." He evidently did not know we were a Band Instrument City, but we did have for many years a very good orchestra at the Bucklen with about eight musicians.

In those days one could go to Mrs. Lusher's restaurant, which operated in Elkhart for ten years, and get a good meal, including, soup, meat, potatoes, vegetables, coffee and pie or ice cream for only 25 cents and we often ate there. At Christmas time she gave a free Christmas dinner to the poor children of Elkhart and as many as 100 came to enjoy one of Mrs. Lusher's good meals. One little girl did not eat her pie and when Mrs. Lusher asked why, the girl remarked: "I am going to take it to my mother." Mrs. Lusher told her to eat it and she would cut another piece for her mother. Mrs. Lusher then fixed up a shoebox with a full lunch in it for the mother and as the little girl carried it away, she held that box as if it contained a fortune.

In laying out additions, John put in his own water mains, sewers and sidewalks, as at that time there was no other way he could do it, as the additions were not built up. When he laid out his Fourth Addition, consisting of four streets, he started with one house on the first lot.

At that period he built about ten houses a year and then left no vacant lots between. If a man came along and wanted to buy a vacant lot just for an investment, he would not sell him the single lot, unless he would agree to build on it, as he figured his addition would look better if a house was on each lot. So this addition had a house on every lot, except one, and that man wanted an extra lot for a nice yard, which was afterwards sodded and kept in nice shape. John also had trees planted between the curb and sidewalk, mostly hard maple trees.

Some of John's men took very much pride in their work and aimed to please. A number of them worked as long as twenty five years for him, as he gave them steady work if they were extra good.

John was always particular about having floors level and if one was not level he knew it immediately, just by walking across a room. All houses in those days had sills, which had to be notched out for the joist. Even where the houses were built in what was afterwards discovered as the high water district, the floors are still level today. He also used patent lath boards to hold plaster, as these boards helped to make a house warmer. They were boards with grooves to hold plaster. One cannot buy this type of lumber today, but they were also good for stability.

John always built a good house until the year 1923. He then built 6 rather cheap houses with no basement, and they sold very quickly. He had a waiting list for more of them, as they were only three rooms in size and sold with lot for $1,000.00. But he stopped building them suddenly, when a friend called to his attention the fact that he would lose his reputation by building such cheap houses, as always before he had built a good house. So no more were built of that type as he did not want to sell an inferior house. They would soon find out that the house was not a good one to live in, as it was far from modern, and a hot house in summer and a cold house in winter. But they sold well because they were cheap.

Many of his regular houses were the same shape and size and he sometimes would build as many as twenty in one year. In this way he could have them built cheaper as there was no lost motion. Each carpenter would know just what to do and would not have to stop and figure, for he had built the same house before a number of times. They had 5 rooms and bath down and 2 rooms upstairs. He liked to build them before he had them sold, as then there were no changes. If he sold the house before it was built the prospect would want more or less changes, which usually made delays and additional costs. In making sales of these properties, 80% were time payment sales and it usually took an average of ten years for them to pay out. Some would pay out faster than the contract called for and some would pay slower than contract terms. Many would fall behind during depression times and would catch up during better times, where some would become discouraged and move out.

One thing in selling a property, especially a new house, he never told the buyer that he was going to sod the lot, unless the buyer would ask that question, in which case he would say yes. But sometimes after the buyer would move in, several loads of black dirt were dumped in the yard and spread after the ground was leveled off. Then several loads of sod would come and the same man who graded the lot would lay the sod, which would take several days. This would always please the buyer, as often they were getting more than they expected and in the long run it was the best way to advertise and even if John overlooked something else, what he had overlooked was seldom mentioned.

A man who later ventured into the real estate business in Florida, before he started, asked John for advice. John told him the above mentioned point and suggested that he, going into a new territory, start out by doing the same. This man built and sold 18 houses in Bradenton, Florida. The local newspaper gave him a writeup and in the article they mentioned this fact, that the real estate man in building up his addition was known as the surprise man, that he never told the buyer all he was going to do, but usually the day before the buyer moved in, a medicine cabinet with an electric fixture over it, went in the wall of the bathroom just over the lavatory at no extra charge to the buyer. The cost of this was not more than $15.00 per house, but it paid dividends right from the start. Though it is not unusual for a real estate dealer to do such a surprise trick, especially when it cost him $15.00, at that time it was something new in Florida.

One time John had a painter working for him and he mentioned to John the following: "I have been a painter for many years, but I have just finished varnishing the woodwork in one of the nicest planned houses I have ever seen." This interested John very much and it was an extra good plan after the painter explained it. "You see," he said, "you have your kitchen, dining room and living room in front on the street, where a woman during the day can see what is going past on the street, as the kitchen sink is right below the window, with shelf on each side, which is where she works. But at night when the travel is going past, the bedrooms are in the back with the bathroom between, where the noise from the street is not apt to disturb one." Each bedroom in this house had an extra large clothes-press which also interested the painter and each bedroom had outside windows on two walls, which was good for ventilation. The house had plenty of electric outlets, so that lamps, radios, sweeper and other appliances could be attached without using the chandeliers.

John once built two houses side by side. One was a square house, the other a long narrow house. Both houses had the same make of furnace. One heated perfectly, the other was just the opposite. After using both furnaces for three years, John accidentally heard about the one house being impossible to heat perfectly, so he sent his furnace man Charles Bruggner to look over the furnace. One glance by Bruggner told the story, as the cold air pipes came down within one inch from the side of the furnace in the narrow house. When the furnace got warm it heated these pipes so the cold air pipes would not work, which resulted in a warm basement and a cold upstairs. After these pipes were changed to a position away from the side of the furnace, it was a perfect heating plant.

Another house John had, the tenant reported the house seemed warm but the tenant was always cold. So Bruggner was sent there too. Here the cold air register was ten inches above the floor on the side wall of the stairway leading upstairs. Bruggner changed this register to the floor and perfect heating was obtained. The coldest air in the room is on the floor but this cold air could not get to the cold air register before it was changed. He also knew if a furnace was too small. He told John once that "one third of your furnace trouble comes from too small a chimney," after which all chimneys built had 11 by 11 tile and the draft on all these chimneys was perfect; a fire can be built much quicker with a good chimney.

One house in Elkhart, centrally located, was known for years as a cold house in winter and during each winter the tenants would move out of it. One day during the summer a local lawyer bought the large house and John reported to him that in winter the house could not be heated satisfactorily. He replied, "I know it, John, but there is a reason. The house has 4 fire places with no dampers in the chimneys, which makes a perfect flow of air from the rooms to the sky 24 hours a day." He was right, for he had the four fire places bricked up and it turned out to be an extra warm house during the winter months. The lawyer lived there the balance of his life.

One cold winter day in February, a tenant in an 8 room house reported he was going to move, on account of having burned 18 tons of coal so far that winter and besides had been cold all winter. John told him that he would

The good old days.

be there at 9 A. M. the next day and he should have a good fire going at that time, as he wanted to see for himself, as the house was a well built one. The tenant had an extra good fire at the time John arrived. He noticed the house was cold when he entered it, and as he held his hand over the register very little warm air was there. But as he opened the basement door, plenty of hot air was in basement, as the castings of the furnace were red hot. John immediately went upstairs and looked around for the cold air register and did not find any. The reason was that the tenant had tacked the carpet down over it. After moving a large bookcase and using a hammer and screwdriver, the carpet was taken up and plenty of heat then flowed from all registers in great abundance. But with it there was smoke, as new castings were needed for the furnace on account of so much overheating.

A man who was starting in the real estate business in Elkhart told John that he was building at that time what he called a model house. "When I get it finished I want you to look it over." Several months later he took John to see it. It was early in spring, and as they entered the front door they noticed that water had been standing on the floor from rain running down the front door and blowing under the door from the wind. This made a bad first impression. A shelter should have been built over the door, which the model house builder had found out by experience in building his first house. The nice brick fireplace had no damper in the chimney. There were no electric outlets for lamps or other appliances, although the house had nice hardwood floors throughout, with hot water heating system, which is the most expensive heating unit, but one of the best. The worst mistake of all was the plumbing. The pipes were run crooked through the basement, and they sagged in places. The kitchen sink was open underneath, and the hot and cold water pipes, including the drain pipe, ran straight through the floor making it hard to clean around. They could have been run through the wall, by making a graceful bend above the floor under the sink. The pipes to the lavatory in the bathroom also ran straight down through the floor, and same with bath tub pipes and water supply pipe to the toilet box. The garage was built about 70 feet from the house, on the alley line, so the car could not go in or out without getting on the vacant lot across the alley. If it had been built closer to the house one would not have had to wade so much snow in winter. The house was an expensive one, but the builder had not given it enough thought to make it a model house. With more forethought he could have improved it 30% with little expense. However, architects make their mistakes, even the best of them.

One time, a well known Elkhart architect was building a nice brick house with tile roof, on the upper St. Joseph River in one of Elkhart's best additions. This architect was good on beauty and has to his credit many nice homes, but he was lacking on small items. The man who was having the house built asked the architect, "What will you charge me to inspect the house every day it is being built, as I want an extra nice job?" The architect replied, "I will do it for 5% additional on the cost of the house," which in the end totaled a large amount, together with the cost of the architect's plans. It however was agreeable, so each day the architect was on the job. After 4 months overseeing the house, it looked as if it were finished, so the owner settled with the architect and began moving in. He bought a new electric refrigerator for the nice tile floor kitchen, but it was then discovered there was no electric outlet for the refrigerator as the architect had never thought of it. So the tile man had to come back and chip out the tile floor not only for an outlet to be installed, but also for a gas pipe to hook up the gas stove, which the architect had also overlooked, plus a vent for the gas stove, as it was an extra large stove and the gas man recommended a vent. So a chimney had to be built for the gas stove after the house was finished. The plans also called for an electric exhaust fan in the kitchen. The architect had also overlooked that, so that was also installed afterwards, making 4 mistakes in one room. As long as the house stands it will show the place where the tile was patched in the kitchen, and the electric fan plainly shows that it was put in after the house was built.

One time John had much trouble with a chimney his mason had built in the center of a large 8 room house. He had sold the house as soon as it was finished but fifteen years later the chimney had settled 4 inches within 2 years. The purchaser came to John for help and John had his men jack up the chimney in the basement, so the floors were level again. But one year later it again had settled the same 4 inches. This time the chimney was jacked up by long timbers and all brick were removed to the bottom of the chimney. Here they found that the original mason had begun the chimney on top of a sawed off stump of a large tree, which stood right where the chimney was to be built. Evidently the original mason thought the stump would never rot; at least it was the easiest way for him to build the chimney. In the long run it would have been much better and cheaper, to have taken the extra time and cut out the stump. A chimney draws much better in winter if it is a warm chimney and when built inside, or in the center of a house, it gives best service and the chimney also helps to heat the house.

But when plastering a room, never plaster over chimney brick. Always place studding around the chimney and lath over, for in this way wallpaper will not wrinkle in the chimney corner as is so often seen in many houses where plaster is against the brick of a warm chimney. In papering a room, many paper hangers never cut the paper for a corner, but plaster the same roll on both walls. It becomes wrinkled in the corner, and the longer it lasts the more it wrinkles. The ideal way is to cut the paper the full length, after measuring the exact space and then paste and apply each piece separately on each wall. In this way the wrinkles will never appear in the corner, no matter how long the paper stays on. It takes a little more time, but particular workmen receive their reward in time and are appreciated by many people who notice such good work. Few workmen are perfect. There are some perfect, but they are scarce. It takes very little more time to do things right than it does to do them wrong. Take for instance an electrician, when he brings the wires to the center of a ceiling for a center light in a room, the fixture should be to the fraction of an inch in the center of that room, then if any fancy papering or steel ceiling work is to be done, the fixture is right where it belongs, so as to match with the squares and the sheet metal worker may begin work in the center of the room. If the fixture is not exactly in the center, it has to be changed in order to be right, at much additional trouble and expense. Another thing in running conduit pipes through house and basement, pipes should be run straight with walls and not crooked. The value of neat work is much appreciated by people who occupy such houses a greater part of their lifetime and when selling a house it makes it much easier to sell perfect workmanship.

One time John ordered a new plumber to do some work in an expensive house that he owned. In running a water pipe and drain from the house to a new garage his only remark to him was: "I want all pipes run as straight and neatly as possible." When the work was inspected two days later, there was not a straight pipe on the new work anywhere, every pipe was crooked. He told the plumber to do the two days work over again, and the plumber was paid in full for the 4 days work. But that plumber from that date on was always a model plumber and when he worked for John afterwards his work was always neat.

One time the sewer got stopped up in front of the office, right under a nice new brick pavement. A large hole had to be made in the paving by taking up the brick and 8 inches of rolled crushed stone underneath. A pile of dirt 3 feet high was dug out all around the hole. When the sewer was fully repaired after the trouble had been located, John said to the man filling the hole, "Throw only one shovel full of dirt at a time and then use the tamper, I will be watching you. Take all the time you want but do it as perfectly as possible, for I don't want a sag in the paving in front of my office." The man spent two full days filling in that hole, tamping dirt and crushed rock, placing one inch of cushion sand between rock and brick, and in laying paving brick and sweeping sand between the brick. No one could afterwards tell that any brick were ever taken up. It is seldom that such common labor is so perfectly done, but it is a pleasure to have workmen of that type. It took far more dirt to fill that hole than he took out.

The slate roof on John's residence made the attic very hot during the summer months, so he had it lathed and plastered. He hired one of his tenants, Ernest Dentz, to mix the plaster. After the plasterer had the work done, Mr. Dentz asked Mrs. Fieldhouse for a mop, pail, scraper, soap and rags, which she gave him. He then went to work and made the floor of the attic look as clean as possible and washed the windows, inside and out. He cleaned up the yard, basement and barn. He seemed to enjoy cleaning, for he mentioned about cleaning all the windows of the house, which he did. John knew he was an extra good man, so he made Dentz a proposition to work, and Dentz worked steady for Mr. and Mrs.

Fieldhouse for 26 years. Mrs. Fieldhouse said to him one day, "Why is it you are so neat about your work?" His reply was that he was the oldest of a family of 8 children, and his mother appointed him to do the housework. The first time he mopped the kitchen floor she made him do it 4 times, before she called it done right. So right there he decided, in the future he would do it right the first time.

During the first world war, Dentz got a telegram from a band instrument factory at Kansas City, offering him a job as burnisher, as some employee there who used to live in Elkhart had recommended him as an extra good man. Dentz immediately went, as the wages offered him were nearly double what he was getting. He usually came back once each year on a visit and he remarked on the first visit, "When I got there the shop was in awful shape, extra dirty throughout, so the second Saturday afternoon I began cleaning the place, working all Saturday night and Sunday. Monday morning the manager wanted to know who was responsible for the cleanup, and the rest of the help pointed to me. They immediately changed my work to clean-up man." He held that job until he died at the age of 83. Dentz looked younger, as he always kept himself neat in appearance.

In having work done such as plumbing, furnace work, electrical work and roof work, John usually hired one firm for each line of work, as in that way he got all small orders, like a leak in a roof, taken care of promptly. If he hired different firms, the chances would be the small orders would not be looked after.

In the year 1902, John Wirley, Trackmaster for the Lake Shore & Michigan Southern Railway Company came in the office and wanted John to go with him the following day to Cleveland, Ohio, to see a Mr. Rockwell of the Railroad Company about buying some land west of Elkhart. At Cleveland they met with Mr. Rockwell who showed them both blueprints of additional land they wanted for new gravity yards, mostly between Elkhart and Osceola, a distance of 4 miles. After spending some time looking over these blueprints, Rockwell asked John, in his opinion, how much the land would cost, to which John replied, "If you let it be known to the public in advance, it will cost about $300,000, if you keep it quiet, it might be bought for $150,000.00. My charge will be 5% for buying it, and I will try to buy it as cheap as possible." John got the job.

Upon arriving in Elkhart he immediately wrote William Bradfield in Chicago, a Northwestern Railway locomotive engineer, who had wanted to buy a farm and had recently written John as to what he had to offer. He wrote Bradfield to come to Elkhart immediately which Bradfield did. Upon arriving John told him to pose as a farm buyer and he

Main Street in Elkhart, 1884.

would pay him for his services. The next morning they both went out early with John's horse and buggy to see as many property owners as they could that day. Mr. Bradfield was just the man for the job, as he was an interested farm buyer, as John had told him that he could have any land left that was not included in the blueprints. Before the sun went down that night, options were obtained on 70% of the land needed for the yards. The next morning word got around among the farmers that something was doing, but none could give the answer. For the remaining 30%, higher prices were paid, but the total net amount the railroad company paid for all land needed was only about $76,000.00, after the land not needed was disposed of, as John in a number of cases bought the entire farm, so the farmer would not know that only a part of his farm was wanted. John kept 76 acres near town himself. Mr. Bradfield bought 70 acres of a Sweitzer farm about 3 miles from Elkhart, where he lived for about 3 years, then sold it at a good profit and went back to railroading on the Northwestern, as his health had greatly improved during his stay on the farm.

The new yards were put in with many parallel tracks, and the railroad venture was successful. Five years later Mr. Rockwell sent for John again. This time it was more than 100 vacant lots with several small houses, which were wanted for new railroad repair shops, as their old shops were built about 30 years before, and now they wanted new modern ones. John soon found that some of the lot owners did not want to sell, so in order to buy their lots from 30 individual owners, John hurriedly platted his 75 acres immediately south of their lots. Then he went to them and offered them two lots for one. Some did business that way, some took the cash, and when John had finished, all the lots and buildings were secured at a cost to the railroad of less than $15,000.00. This pleased Rockwell so much that he offered John a job of buying any land needed by them between Chicago and Buffalo, but John refused, as he had his real estate in Elkhart, which usually kept him busy.

The railroad company first built a large electric power house, put in sewers, and built a tunnel 800 feet long to connect a total of 14 buildings they had intended to build. But the work was stopped on account of the depression of 1907 and the new shops were never built at Elkhart.

During the depression of 1930 our old railroad shops were abandoned and the workers were transferred to Collinwood, Ohio, with many of them still working there. This loss of the shops was felt by Elkhart for many years. The Fieldhouse West Side Addition would have been a successful addition, had the new shops been built in Elkhart, but because they were not built here the addition was not a success. In nearly fifty years there are less than fifty buildings in the addition consisting of 343 lots. If the shops had been built as planned, it might have been a far different story, as the employees could have lived near their work.

In 1907 when this addition was platted and staked out there were 9 streets. John Fieldhouse bought an even 1,000 hard maple trees to be set out in this addition early in the spring. Each tree was at least two inches through at the trunk and ten or more feet in height. John was there to see that they were planted right and that the dirt was properly tamped around the roots of each tree. But where he should have been was where the trees were being dug, for instead of digging the trees out as he supposed they were, with hand shovel, the men were pulling the trees out of the ground with a team of horses, by wrapping a blanket around the trunk of the tree, near the ground, around which they would wrap a rope several times, the other end attached to the whippletree. When the team would pull hard enough by being whipped a little, the roots of the tree would be pulled from the ground. It took a great amount of work to plant 1,000 trees, but 80% of them died. If they had been dug with a shovel, the loss would not have exceeded 10%, for John had them cultivated the first year to give them proper moisture. When the surface soil is broken, the moisture from below does not evaporate, as it does if not broken, as there is a small amount of moisture from below coming through the ground all the time.

It was noticed later that the bark peeled off one side of each tree, near the ground, which was full proof that the trees had been pulled and the seller of the trees finally admitted it, when he was shown the dead trees. The trees that did survive turned out to be beautiful, and had they all lived, the addition would have been very beautiful today as the trunk sizes will average around ten inches in diameter. When full grown the maple tree is one of the most beautiful trees in this country.

One time a man from Detroit called in the office and inquired the way to Detroit. He mentioned that his wife and he had started from Detroit two years before in a house trailer sixteen feet long, with the intention of visiting every State in the Union. They would have completed the mission when they got back to Detroit, 172 miles away. When John asked him which state was the most beautiful, he replied: "What state do you think?" John said: "Colorado?" The stranger said: "Indiana." John said: "Why is Indiana?" to which the stranger replied: "Colorado has the mountains, but those mountains do not have the hard maple trees."

Dr. Menges, an Elkhart dentist, purchased for several hundred dollars a seven acre tract of land about 2 miles north of Elkhart with Christiana Creek running through the property. On the creek bank the doctor had built a very small cottage costing not more than $1,000.00. He planted numerous trees on the property, including 7 different kinds of evergreens. Christiana Creek never goes dry, as it is fed by about twenty different lakes and is a stream about thirty feet wide. After the doctor had lived there a number of weeks each summer for 7 years, a South Bend, Indiana, man and wife one day came to look over the landscape when the doctor was there. They asked the doctor many questions and after their third visit in 3 weeks, they wanted to buy the property. The doctor did not want to sell, as his wife was much attached to it. The South Bend man finally made a cash offer of $10,000.00 for the property of 7 acres, which the doctor refused. The South Bend man then stated that he and his wife had toured in all directions from South Bend for a residential building site. "On account of your trees, doctor, we like your place the best." Nothing improves residential property as much as trees, however they should not be placed too near the house, as they later darken the window, and the roots fill sewer tile, unless iron soil pipe is used.

John Fieldhouse always set out hard maple trees in his additions and Jim Williams from

Adamsville was usually the man who set them out, and took great pride in doing it. He would usually get half a load of good black dirt for around the roots and in digging a tree out, he was very particular to get most all the roots. He would always plant them one half foot deeper than he dug them out, and would always put a dab of paint on the north side of the trunk before he dug them, then he would set that paint spot toward the north. He would dig them out with a shovel and as he set them out he would tamp the dirt well around the roots. He would water them for the first two years through dry periods. Jim Williams seldom lost a tree.

A home owner came in the office one day to find out why his two front lawn trees died. They were hard maple, which he bought from a farmer, who guaranteed them to grow, provided they were watered frequently, which they were. They were 4 inches through and were set out by the farmer, but after a year and a half they were both dead. So the farmer replaced each with three inch trees, telling the property owner that the first trees were too large to transplant. The propery owner watered the second set of trees diligently, but in a year and a half they were both dead, so the farmer made good the third time with two inch trees and in less than two years they were both dead. John told him that the farmer had probably failed to bring enough roots.

He advised him to forget that farmer and get trees of someone else and to be firm with the man to get all the roots, which he did and today he has two nice trees but they are not as large as he would have liked to have them. He would have had much larger trees if the first man had brought more of the roots.

In the spring and fall are the only times trees should be set out and not during the hot summer months or cold winter months. Jim Williams always covered the roots with canvas to keep the heat of the sun off of them, as well as the cold, which was another reason he was successful with his trees. It was not luck, it was good judgment.

When I was a boy I enjoyed planting tree seeds and had much enjoyment in watching them grow from year to year. It was no work at all to plant a seed and I planted many walnuts, but of course some did not come up and produce a tree but those that did are today large beautiful trees. My first experience in planting seeds was when I was about 12 years old. I saw some maple seeds on our lawn, so I planted three seeds at different spots covering them with a small amount of dirt. I forgot about them but several years later I noticed three trees growing in the lawn and recalled planting the seed. Today the trunks of those trees are more than 14 inches through and the trees are well over fifty feet tall, all from three small seeds. The trees are still growing and no doubt will continue to do so for many years after I am gone with the wind.

If you buy a lot today, plant your favorite trees on it, at the right season of the year when the leaves are off. It will give you much pleasure to watch them grow and it will make a more beautiful place to live. One may take any vacant property and improve it with trees, fruit trees for instance. It takes a Northern Spy apple tree 15 years to bear fruit from the date it is started, but most people do not look that far ahead. Years have a habit of slipping past and when we take a backward glance we wonder where they went. If you have no trees to show or look at, you have missed something on life's highway. The easiest and best way to plant a tree is from the seed, as it adapts itself to all conditions and needs less attention, because it is grown the natural way. There are many people who destroy trees, who never plant any. There is no better monument to have along highways and streams than trees, planted for people to enjoy for many years. Even if you plant them from seed, they are apt to grow, at least some of them. If you plant a few each year you will have some pleasure through life watching them grow. In some locations, where trees are not cared for, they are sometimes disfigured by the limbs or branches on the trunk of the tree growing too near the ground. In other words the trees need trimming and some of them are on Boulevards in our cities within a stone's throw of some of our newest and nicest residences. If you are the owner of one of these lots, or live near them and want to do a good deed for the day, trim up those branches close to the trunk of the tree. Trim high enough so one may walk under the tree, and you will have done your part in making your neighborhood more beautiful. Don't forget to pile the brush in a small neat pile, which will show that someone did a good deed as sometimes a good deed is very much appreciated. He who leaves a pile of beer cans, waste paper or glass bottles along a roadside is no gentleman.

On one of our farm properties, at a ditch along the road, someone dumped about three bushel baskets full of tin cans, glass bottles and waste materials and it disfigured the scenery considerably. A man who passed the place twice each day stopped his automobile and looked over the trash. In it he discovered a grocery bill giving the man's name and address. He handed the information to us, so we notified the man we would give him just 48 hours to clean that mess up or he would be prosecuted, and the mess promptly disappeared. The man was not told how we got our information and we presume he wondered how we found out it was he.

Once we had forty acres not far from Elk-

Main street in Elkhart 1887. Notice one horse drawn street car. In 1890, Elkhart was the first city in the State of Indiana to have electric operated street cars.

hart, where fully 100 loads of trash and ashes had been dumped in five years time, right on level ground. Several hundred feet away was a small house, so we notified the occupant we would give a reward for the license number of any truck dumping ashes on our property. In three days we had information that a three yard truck dumped about 9 yards of ashes on this land, so we obtained the name and address of the owner of the truck and we went to see him one evening. We told him we would give him one week to remove those nine yards of ashes. They were all removed by him shoveling them himself on his extra high truck, and never again were any more ashes or rubbish dumped there.

I used to travel a road often where a street sign on a metal post was slanting at a 20% angle, so one day I stopped with our truck and spent about twenty minutes digging down three feet and straightening the sign. It has been perfectly straight ever since and that was years ago. The location was built up solid with nice residences, but no one living there evidently ever thought about straightening that post.

One time about 1903 John was going to South Bend on the interurban car and Frank Brumbaugh, a local citizen and agent for the Bellefontaine Bridge Company of Bellefontaine, Ohio, was on the car in the same seat with John. John said to Frank: "Why don't you build your bridges in Elkhart?" Frank said: "I would if I had $15,000.00." John said: "Would that be all it would take? One bridge might cost $15,000.00." Frank said: "It might, but the steel could be bought on credit and paid for after the bridge was finished." John said: "Be at my office, Frank, at 4 o'clock this afternoon."

When John got back he phoned everyone he could think of, and at 4 P. M. when Frank walked in the back room of John's office, there were sixteen men to meet him. John told them the story of what was said on the interurban and also stated: "Let us build a bridge plant in Elkhart. H. E. Bucklen will donate five acres of ground for such a factory and Bucklen will also take some stock." William Pratt said: "I will take $1,000.00 worth of stock." Each man in the room agreed to take the same amount, and the Elkhart Bridge Company was started. The Bridge Company has been turning out iron and steel bridges ever since. It is a good institution today, and occupies every square foot of the five acres in making bridges, although at one time, if it had not been for some tornado insurance, the factory might have been lost.

About 1907 John and his wife were on a pleasure trip in Buffalo and there was such a strong wind-storm that it blew a large boat from Lake Erie onto dry land. When John got back to Elkhart, I met them at the train

and his first question was: "Is the Bridge
Plant's large building still standing?" My
answer was: "Yes." He said: "Place $5,000
tornado insurance on it and send Brumbaugh
the bill." John at that time had a mortgage
on the property and wanted to be fully pro-
tected. Frank Brumbaugh would not pay for
the tornado insurance. He said, the building
could not blow down, as the machine belting
alone would keep it from blowing down, so
John paid the premium himself in order to
protect his mortgage.

About three years later, one Sunday afternoon, Elkhart had an extra hard windstorm
and the large building was blown to the
ground. But John did not know about it until
the next morning, when an early caller at the
office told him what had happened, and also
stated there was not one part of the building
five feet above ground level. One hour later
in came Frank Brumbaugh, a sick looking
man. His first remark was: "John, that tornado insurance you spoke to me about several years ago, is that in force yet?" John
said: "How do you suppose it could be in
force, when you did not pay the premium?
Do you expect miracles to happen?" Frank
said: "Did you know that the Bridge Building
blew down yesterday?" John said: "Yes."
Brumbaugh was almost in tears, for he knew
that John had a mortgage on the property,
and there was not much left. In half an hour

Brumbaugh left the office to get on his bicycle, a sad look on his face. John called to him, "Frank, that tornado insurance is in full force." Frank was overjoyed, and came back and stayed another half hour. The insurance adjuster agreed it was a total loss and paid the $5,000.00 promptly. With this $5,000.00 a new building was built and the company made bridges that summer with no roof over their machinery, while the new building was being built.

Frank Brumbaugh was later killed in an automobile accident and the name of the company was changed to Elkhart Bridge & Iron Co. They celebrated their 50th anniversary in July, 1954. During this period of time the company built a total of 3,500 bridges, in 30 states and Canada, including the first steel bridges for both the Indiana and Michigan highway departments. The firm's first venture into the fabrication of steel for building was in 1907 for the First National Bank of Gary, when the great Gary Steel Mills had just begun to take shape. Among the steel buildings fabricated by the firm in Elkhart are the North Side Gym, Citric Acid Plant of Miles Laboratories, American Coating Mills division plant, Excel Corporation and Chicago Telephone Supply plants.

John always liked manufacturing and had stock in a number of different Elkhart industries. He had about $15,000.00 worth of stock

in the Davis Acetylene Company of Elkhart
for about 15 years and during this period
never received a dividend. Mr. Davis, the
President, was for some reason mad at one
of the stockholders and took all the profits
for his salary and was not fair with his part-
ners. Davis however invented an acetylene
welder which was very good for certain work.
When the large boat "Eastland" tipped over
in the Chicago River and more than 800 people drowned on account of it, it was the Davis
Acetylene Welder that cut out plates of steel
in the side of the boat. When the boat was
repaired, the same plates were welded back
and hardly a mark remained to indicate a repair. Shortly after this, Davis sent his head
man around to the stockholders and offered
them par for their stock. They were all willing to sell. Had they said no, they would
have been far richer, as the plant was immediately moved to New Jersey, after which they
made millions of dollars. Davis was on the
inside and some of the stockholders were on
the outside.

One of the most important factory invest-
ments made by John was about 1904 when
Charles A. Sidway from Chicago called at
the office late one afternoon. He was a young
man 27 years of age and had just $500.00 in
cash. Harden Markel, who owned a two
story building 40 by 80 feet, had offered to
let Sidway have the building for one year for

$500.00 rent, paid in advance. He offered to throw in some contents of the building, which he had bought from a receiver of a company that had failed in business making bedside tables. Sidway was a stranger, but a very good talker. He wanted John to loan him $500.00 on his personal note for one year and with the money he would start up and finish the unmanufactured goods. He made such a good appearance, and would not take no for an answer that at 10 P. M. John agreed to loan him the $500.00 the following day. Sidway got it and with it he operated the plant for a period of one year. On the same day a year later, at 9 o'clock in the morning, he appeared with a check for the full amount of the $500.00 plus $30.00 interest, which gave John great confidence in the young man. John afterwards loaned Sidway money a good many times and Sidway always paid on the due date.

Several years later Sidway noticed one of his employees by the name of Timmerhoff working at his bench during the noon hour and right away he was interested in seeing what the man was doing. Timmerhoff told him that he had a daughter who lived one half mile from the city street car line, and he lived one half mile from the opposite end of the car line, and as his daughter had a two year old child, he was making a cart for the child that would fold up, so that his daughter could carry it on the street car. Sidway told him to forget his other work and keep working on the gocart, which he did. After it was completed, Sidway helped him secure a patent on the gocart.

The Sidway Company started to manufacture the gocart, allowing Timmerhoff five cents royalty on each one turned out. The factory began to grow like a mushroom. Addition after addition was built connecting with the original plant, as Sidway later bought the plant from Markel. A few years later the Sidway Company was manufacturing as high as 800 gocarts a day. Sidway was a worker, and was at the plant at 7 each morning and did not leave until 7 at night. At the height of the company's success he died. At the time of his death he was receiving a salary of $15,000.00 a year and was only 37 years old.

After Sidway's death a Mr. Pete Kendall stepped into his place, Kendall was an auditor. Shortly afterwards he wanted Sidway's salary, to which John objected, as John now owned 1,600 shares out of 2,500 shares of Sidway stock. When Kendall failed to get the salary he wanted, he got an eastern factory to buy John's stock, for which they offered $150.00 per share as follows: Pay cash for half and pay preferred stock for the other half. The deal was so made and John, in making his income tax return, reported profit on the cash received, but made no report of the stock.

When the U. S. Internal Revenue man checked John's return for that year, he revamped the report and threw in the trade also, making over $18,000 additional income taxes, with penalty included. When John received the bill for this amount, he wrote them he wanted a hearing in Washington on the subject, so they gave him a date two months ahead and John was there on that date. The government men insisted that their man was right, but John argued he wasn't. After several hours arguing, John got off on another subject. He said to them: "I have a house and a large lot on the St. Joseph River in Elkhart, a beautiful place now vacant, and my cost runs to about $22,000.00. I know a man by the name of Johnson who is near 70 years of age, who has a 400 acre farm in Michigan that I would like to have. You are income tax men. Now suppose that I would trade places even with him, no cash difference, so that he can retire and have a nice place to live. How much would my income tax be on a trade like that?" The men said: "If it was an even trade, there would be no tax until you sold the farm. Then the cost of the farm would be the cost of the house; if you sold it for more, the difference would be your profit, if you sold it for less, then you could take a loss." John then said: "That is just what I

thought you would say. Now explain to me
the difference in trading 800 shares of common stock for 1,200 shares of preferred
stock." The men made no reply until one of
them said, "Well, Mr. Fieldhouse, I guess you
are right. You being a trader, there won't be
any tax in your case until you sell the preferred stock or until it is redeemed by the
company." That was the end of a long con-
troversy.

John had many a battle with U. S. Income
tax men. The Elkhart Chamber of Commerce
had a drive about 1926 for funds to bring in
new factories, which they did later on. John
having considerable real estate by that time,
in order to increase its value, and do good
for Elkhart, gave a total of $15,000.00 He lat-
er deducted this from his income tax figures
as advertising expense and right away this
figure was thrown out. Again John asked for
a date and this time the place was Indianapolis.

Before going to Indianapolis, John went
over his books and marked down all the different factories he had done business with
during his real estate career. All those he had
stock in and all those he had loaned money
to, and all that he had sold property to. There
was a total of 54 names when the list was
finished. While the argument lasted all day,
the final verdict was in John's favor. But if
he had not had that list, he would have lost

Fieldhouse office in 1905.

the battle. John made considerable money in manufacturing concerns, but he lost considerable money also, for they were not all successes. But he liked to do business, and Elkhart was always a good manufacturing city, with a variety of factories. He often said, "A man who never makes a loss, never does very much business," And he also said, "A man once got rich by not buying at the lowest price or selling at the highest price." It was the game that he liked, and that was one reason that he worked many hours a day.

As a rule John never missed a show at the Bucklen Theatre. He usually had the same seats and liked to see some of the shows over and over again, as some of them came year after year. He was Agent for Herbert E. Bucklen, who was the best customer that John ever had. The Bucklen Hotel and Bucklen Theatre were named after him. John was Bucklen's agent for many years, having sold him at different times considerable Elkhart property, Bucklen always said when he bought it, "I will take it, John, if you will look after it for me."

Bucklen got his start in an Elkhart Drug Store back in 1870. He clerked in the store, and when anyone brought in a prescription to be filled, Bucklen took a copy of it. At the end of several years, Bucklen had what he considered four very good ones, so he gave each one a name and stocked up on each. He advertised in the paper about his medicine, and as he sold some, he advertised more. As his business grew, he took in other towns and cities, and stocked his medicine in their stores. He soon moved to Chicago, and continued the same business from there.

One night John noticed at 10 o'clock Bucklen had a democrat wagon filled with wooden signs advertising his medicines. Bucklen asked him if he wanted to go with him on a moonlight ride. He told John that he could hold the lines while he, Bucklen, would nail the signs on fences along the country roads advertising his medicines. Bucklen told John the next day he was up all night putting up his signs. Bucklen was working while the other fellow was sleeping and it paid dividends for Bucklen.

When Bucklen died in 1918 he was worth more than five million dollars, but he made considerable money buying Chicago real estate and holding onto it. H. E. Bucklen did much for Elkhart and gave free ground to new industries locating here, for he had a lot of confidence in the city. He bought much Elkhart real estate and he bought the greater part of it from his old friend, John Fieldhouse.

About 1888 Bucklen built a steam railroad between Elkhart and Mishawaka, ten miles in length and in doing this, he connected switch tracks to many Elkhart industries.

He operated this road for nearly ten years
and then sold it to the Lake Shore & Michigan Southern Railroad, now known as New
York Central, at a profit of $250,000.00, and
it was an extra good buy for the Railroad Co.
Today it is the best paying ten miles of road
in the New York Central system. This is
largely on account of the Indiana & Michigan Electric Company power plant near
Mishawaka, which burns about forty car-
loads of coal a day. All coal used at this power plant is delivered over this ten miles of
track.

After H. E. Bucklen sold the railroad, the
profit enticed him to start an interurban road
from Elkhart to Toledo. This line was afterwards a loss to his Estate of over a million
dollars. The road was sold by a receiver during the first World War and the rails were
taken up and shipped to France. The coming
of automobiles was affecting interurban roads
all over the country. About the year 1911 interurban roads all over the country were doing a good business, but the automobile afterwards put most of them out of business and
very few are operating today.

After Bucklen's death in 1918, John bought
much of the Elkhart real estate, including
Hotel Bucklen and the Bucklen Theatre. He
also sold for the Estate a total of nine farms
owned by Bucklen, North of Elkhart.

Bucklen was one of the busiest men and
always had a surplus of ambition. During the

Centennial Fair at Philadelphia back in 1876, Bucklen established a soda fountain at the Fair and operated it himself. At that time soda fountains were new to everyone. He had established one before in one corner of his father's drug store at Main and Jackson Streets in Elkhart.

When John was agent for Bucklen, every three months he would send in a statement covering 38 properties we had charge of and each property was named and numbered. The main sheet told the story of the debit and credit of each property. The remaining sheets showed the rents received from each tenant and listed all items paid out. Then there was a separate bundle of receipts for all items paid out. Bucklen never had much to say about the reports, but John heard through the grapevine route that one time he showed one of the reports to his Chicago agent and instructed him to make all future reports the same way as "Fieldhouse makes his," so Bucklen could understand them.

Bucklen lived in Chicago next to his laboratory, a six story building. One night the laboratory building caught on fire in the back part. There was a fire wall in the center of the building. Bucklen was in the street when the fire department came. He said to the Chief, "Get a man in the front tower with a hose as quickly as possible and then he can keep the fire from coming over the center wall." The Chief replied, "I would not go in that tower myself and would not ask any of my men to." Bucklen then shouted so all could hear, "I will give the first man who enters that tower with a hose, $200.00." In three minutes a man was there with a fire hose. The entire back part of the building was destroyed, but the front part was saved. Bucklen knew what to say and how to say it. When Bucklen died he owned more acres of land inside the city limits of Chicago than any other man; he invested heavily in real estate.

During and after the First World War the Fieldhouse Real Estate Office was very busy. We had many rental properties to look after and many collections on monthly contracts, and John kept building new houses from year to year, selling most of them on payments. During this time he built as many as 20 houses a year. By working early and late, and having good health, he was a busy man, and he enjoyed work. However, about 1924 he discovered that he could buy contracts from other agents and real estate men at a discount for cash, which would relieve him from building houses.

He later found that some of these houses were not built as well in many ways and far more fault was found by the dissatisfied contracting buyers and they sometimes had good reasons for finding fault. For instance one of the builders would say to a carpenter, "How much will you charge for doing all the carpenter work on this plan of house?" The carpenter, wanting the job, would bid low. Then in shingling the house he would drive just one nail in each shingle. If he had driven 3 nails in each shingle the shingle roof would have lasted 25 years, without leaking. But with one nail some shingles would blow off in ten years, causing a leak. The proof was found by picking up a shingle which had blown off and finding only one nail hole in it.

When John sold a house direct he would ask the customer quite a number of questions, as to where he worked, how long he had worked there, how much money he had to pay down and whether he had saved it out of his wages or if he had borrowed the first payment to pay down. John usually asked a few such questions before he made out the contract, for he wanted to know if the buyer knew how to save money.

There are some people who cannot or do not know how to save money, for their eyes are larger than their pocketbooks. During the depression days from 1929 to 1936 John took back fully 100 homes that he thought were sold before the depression started, and a large percentage of the homes he took back were those on the contracts he had bought from other real estate men. Those he had sold direct held on, and afterwards paid out, with few exceptions.

During this depression John at one time in

1932 had 38 vacant houses and at the same time had 5 vacant store rooms. Some of the houses stood vacant as long as 3 years and during that period he seldom had a call for a house. Not only that, he had many houses where the contracting buyers were not making any payments, or the tenants were not paying any rent. Often people came in and wanted to occupy vacant houses and not pay any rent. They would say, "Isn't it better for your house to be occupied, than to stand vacant?"

After the depression days, John decided it was better for a house to stand vacant, as far as the owner was concerned. For he found the tenants he let stay longest without paying any rent, when he did finally ask them to move, would not move without an argument. One who owed $308.00 at $9.00 per month rental, made this remark, "You set me out of the house, Mr. Fieldhouse, and I will knock your block off." Another tenant who owed $260.00 made this remark, "I have six children, Mr. Fieldhouse, and I think you should give us shelter, same as you have in the past." Each of these made John all the trouble they could. Each did considerable damage to the property in the way of driving spikes in the walls, as if they were driven to hang pictures. By letting them stay too long, John lost their friendship, but in many cases it was different. Of all the delinquent rent due us after the tenants moved, less than 5% was ever collected. John often said, "I can go out and make money easier than I can go out and try to collect past due rent accounts."

John one time in closing a deal, overpaid a man in another city $260.00. He gave him a check for $4,000.00, where it should have been $3,740.00. He wrote the man regarding it fully six times during a two year period, but received no reply. John forgot about the transaction until a friend told him the man was laughing about how he outdid Fieldhouse. This made John do some hard thinking, as he hated to be outdone by what he termed a crook. So he wrote the man a seventh letter something like this: "As you have failed to answer my six previous letters, I feel that I should at least be fair with you and let you know what my present plan is. You have not paid me what you owe me, so I presume you do not pay others. Within thirty days from date, I will write the U. S. Internal Revenue Department and inform them that you beat me out of $260.00 and that you personally made a certain profit two years ago on the same deal, and if they look up your income tax return for that year, they will probably find that that profit was not listed. If not, they should bill you for it." A check for $260.00 came by return mail made out to Johw W. Fieldhouse.

It was a little like a clerk in the Indiana Hotel in Elkhart. He was suspicious of a man stopping at the hotel, and had him sized up as a crook, so he had the bellboy follow him to his automobile more than a block away from the hotel and write down his auto license number, which the clerk placed on file. The man had registered from Fort Wayne. After staying three weeks at the hotel, one day the man did not return and there was room rent for three weeks past due. So the clerk wrote to Indianapolis for the name and address of the auto owner. It was Terre Haute, Indiana, instead of Fort Wayne. He immediately wrote the man for the three weeks bill and received a check for the full amount by return mail.

John also rented the Hotel Bucklen for ten years to a George Sherman, who was a very good hotel man. One day a man registered as G. W. Gwilt, and at the time he registered he told Sherman that he would like to deposit a diamond ring in the hotel safe, as he intended to marry an Elkhart girl in thirty days, and he did not want to take up the ring until the day of the wedding.

He lived like a king around the hotel for thirty days and got his meals there and charged them to his room. He came in John's real estate office and borrowed his horse and buggy to show his girl a property John had shown him, all of which he told Sherman. He evidently picked up a girl, for the girl's mother noticed the certain stranger was driving John Fieldhouse's rig, which gave the girl's mother confidence in the young man.

Fieldhouse office in 1904.

The young man, to give George Sherman confidence, brought the young lady to the hotel several times for dinner, which additional bill was also added to the room rent.

The day before the date of the wedding, Gwilt gave Sherman a check for the entire thirty days hotel bill. The check was large enough that he received $50.00 change, for George Sherman still had the diamond ring in the safe, which would not be called for until the next day. That time never came. The check was later returned as no good and when George opened the box containing the ring, there was a nickel in it, which made about the same weight as a ring. George Sherman never forgot G. W. Gwilt to his last day; he had been fooled before, but never so badly.

One day a nice appearing man stopped at the Truex Hotel for a stay of three days. This man visited the Night Rider Garage and arranged to buy the tenant out by hiring him to work for him as a sheet metal worker, as he was going to use the 20,000 square feet of floor space of the building as an air conditioning sales and work shop for Elkhart County. He was going to sell air conditioning to industrial plants, hotels and theatres on a large scale. The next thing he wanted was a five year lease on the building in his name. Henderson brought him to the office and a new five year lease was made in the stranger's name. With this lease plus his smooth line of talk, he showed the lease to Truex, so Truex cashed a $50.00 check for him. He then went to the Hotel Bucklen to see about permanent rooms for himself and wife, and got another $50.00 check cashed after showing the lease. That was not all. He did not ask John Fieldhouse, but he did ask three other business places to cash his check for $50.00 after showing them his lease covering the Night Rider Garage and telling them an extra good fairy tale about how he was going to patronize them when they arrived in Elkhart. His wife was with him on all his calls. His checks were worthless, and he left before three days with the greater share of $250.00 net profit by his short visit in Elkhart. He did not even pay his hotel bill.

The banner story happened during the first World War, when one summer day, an elderly, good looking, well dressed man called at the office and wanted the price of the Inner Brace Furniture Company, a factory John had for sale for a wealthy man named E. C. Nichols, who wanted to retire from business. The plant was for sale at $200,000.00. John took the stranger out to the plant and he and Nichols took him through the large factory, spending several hours wih him. He seemed interested and stated he would call again in a few days, which he did, bringing with him two other well dressed men. The three went through the plant, spending a full half day. The one man, Joseph Weil, seemed the most business like. He wanted to inspect Mr. Nichols' books, which he did, after which the three left by train for Chicago.

Several days later, the three men called again, bringing with them three more men and after all had inspected the plant, they again left for Chicago. Mr. Nichols was sure they were going to take the property, but John told Nichols they were not going to take it. John told Nichols there was something strange about these men, that to him they did not seem like buyers. In a few days two other men came to look over the plant and these men stayed a full day. Several days after they had gone Mr. Joseph Weil phoned John Fieldhouse and wanted him and Mr. Nichols to come to Chicago to close the deal. But John bolted. He told Weil that he did not do business in Illinois, that he only did it in Indiana. But Weil hung on and wanted them to come, for the reason, he said, there were many people involved in the deal. That the head man did not want to come to Elkhart, as he was sickly and did not want to travel. But John insisted that he also did not want to travel, and said, "It is in Elkhart at my office, or no sale." Several days later a fine looking well dressed man called at the office, claimed he had just stopped off going through to Chicago from New York ·City, and wanted John to go along with him. John told him that Elkhart was the only place he did business, for John was suspicious and was really afraid to go, much to the disgust of Mr. Nichols, who blamed John for not working to his interest.

After several days Weil and one of the men came in, claiming they had driven down from Chicago and wanted to know if John and Nichols would meet them at the Oliver Hotel in South Bend the next day. John said, "No, here, or no deal." That was the last John saw of Weil. Weil was a very nice appearing man, did not get the least bit excited and seemed very friendly.

About six months later the Chicago papers gave an extensive writeup regarding Joseph Weil. They claimed he had, at the same time that he was calling on John, swindled a Kokomo man out of $120,000.00, and a Fort Wayne man out of $60,000.00. This did not surprise John, but it did Nichols. John sized the bunch up as no buyers, he knew they were up to something, but he did not know what.

Weil and some of the rest of his gang were sent to prison. He remained for years, but he was released before his term was up, as he was claimed to be a model prisoner. John wanted to know how he had swindled the Kokomo man out of $120,000.00. He afterwards found out and this was the way Weil did it. Some of Weil's pals went to the Kokomo man and said that they wanted to buy his steel mill in Kokomo. After looking the plant over they induced him to take the afternoon train for Chicago. On the train they met Weil in one of the Pullmans. The men knew Weil and introduced him to the Kokomo man. On the Pullman seat was a popular magazine with Joseph Weil's picture on the front cover. Weil wore a Van Dyke beard, which made him look distinguished and the Kokomo man noticed the picture resembled Weil. He read under the picture "Mr. Joseph Weil, who received a salary of $100,000.00 a year as chemist for the Standard Oil Company."

When they got to Chicago they went to Joseph Weil's office where there were ten stenographers. Weil invited the Kokomo man to go with him to dinner, after which Weil took him to a show. After the show Weil took him to a hotel where they talked in the Kokomo man's room. Weil told him he had just returned from New York City, where he had secured an old stockholders list of a copper mine in Arizona. The company had failed and the Standard Oil Company had ordered him to drill for oil on the land where a copper mine had been years before. Weil said they got no oil, although they went down several thousand feet, but they had gone through rich beds of copper, about 20 feet below where the former miners had stopped digging. He had found the name of a Chicago party, who owned 3,000 shares of this old copper mine stock and he suggested that the Kokomo man call on the party and if possible, buy the stock for him. The Kokomo man was willing to do it and early the next morning Weil gave him $10,000.00 in currency and the address in North Chicago. The Kokomo man hired a taxi and found the man and his wife living there. After spending some time talking with them, he bought the old stock from them for $3,500.00 cash and then went back to Weil's office, where Weil was anxiously waiting. Weil was so pleased, that he gave the Kokomo man $3,500 cash for his trouble. After the other factory meeting the Kokomo man went home with his $3,500.00. If he had stopped then with Weil, he would have been $3,500.00 ahead.

Within a week Weil walked in the Kokomo man's office and told him that about 30 miles south of Kokomo he had discovered a man who owned 12,000 shares of the stock and if Weil secured that, he would have full control of the old copper mine and could later buy the balance of the stock. He wanted the Kokomo man to go to this man and buy the stock and he would go along with him.

They took the Kokomo man's car and drove the thirty miles. They found the man was a farmer, working on his farm. He told them the copper mine stock had cost his father $120,000.00 and he would never sell it for less than that amount for his father had always said there was copper there. After they left the farmer, Weil was crazy to buy the stock, for it meant riches for him. They drove to Kokomo and Weil phoned his Chicago bank-

er, only to find that he had just left for Detroit. He asked the Kokomo man if he would
loan him the amount needed and promised
to give him an interest in the project. The
farmer had mentioned another party had
written him about the stock and the man was
coming to see him about it. The Kokomo
man agreed, so they went back and bought
the stock. Weil told him to keep the stock
and come to Chicago the next day for his
money. He went, but found Weil's office vacant. Then he went to the house in North
Chicago, only to find that the house had been
rented furnished for only one week, so it was
a total $120,000.00 loss to the Kokomo man,
less the $3,500.00.

The Kokomo man was not lonesome, there
were others. One man in Fort Wayne lost
$60,000.00 and another in Grand Rapids lost
more than that, about the same time that
Weil was working on John Fieldhouse.

Weil was aferwards caught and sent to
prison with several others of his crew. After
he was in prison for awhile, the Court needed
him as a witness, so a deputy took him to
Chicago. As they were going to the train on
the return trip, Weil wanted to go into a
store. As they entered, Weil told the clerk
that he wanted a good hat a certain size,
which he got and paid for, while the deputy
stood by. That hat was for the Warden of
the penitentiary. In less than three years

Weil was walking the streets again, a free man.

In January, 1915, John made a trip by train with his wife and son to Florida and in Miami, stopped at the Halcyon Hotel. Miami at that time had only 12,000 population and there was no city called Miami Beach. There was only one house and one swimming pool on Miami Beach Island, which was 6 miles long and a mile wide. Across the street from the Halcyon Hotel was a large ten room frame dwelling painted white with green blinds, with palm trees between the curb and the sidewalk, the residence of Dr. Jackson. Behind this house on the same lot was Dr. Jackson's office. The lot was 100 feet on Flagler Street by 140 feet deep on Second Avenue. A sign was on it "For Sale." One evening John asked the doctor, who was sitting on his porch, "Doctor, what price do you ask for the property?" He replied, "$25,000.-00." John looked the property over and before he left that evening he offered the doctor $20,000.00 for it. The doctor did not answer for a half minute, but finally said, "No. $25,-000.00 is my lowest price and my only reason for selling is, I have two daughters and I don't like the schools down here."

John afterwards heard that Miami was growing. In 1915 there was a depression down there on account of the war in Europe; the grapefruit and oranges were rotting on

the ground in the outlying groves. John oft-
en wondered about Dr. Jackson's property
and asked several people who had later made
trips to Miami about it, but no one seemed to
know what John was talking about.

About 1919 a former Elkhartan named Mc-
Laughlin came back to Elkhart on a visit. Mc-
Laughlin lived in Miami, so John asked him
about Dr. Jackson and his property. Mc-
Laughlin knew Dr. Jackson and stated he
was still occupying the property, so John
asked him what he thought that property
was worth and McLaughlin said he thought
it would sell for $100,000.00, as it was the best
corner in Miami. John had counted in 1915,
at 2 o'clock in the afternoon, 102 people had
passed the property in 5 minutes and he said
to me, "That is business property." Three
years later McLaughlin returned again and
said Dr. Jackson had leased the property to
a moving picture concern, who, after Dr.
Jackson moved the house and office, built a
theatre building called the Hippodrome,
which cost $45,000.00. He gave them a 20
year lease at $9,000.00 a year rental. Dr.
Jackson a few years later paid the moving
picture people $294,00.00 to cancel the lease,
and then sold the property for an even
$1,000,000.00. John afterwards remarked that
if he had bought the property for $25,000.00,
the chances would have been, he would have
sold out as soon as he had made a good profit.

John went to Florida again in 1923, and in

The barn home of Gyp and Topsy, back of Fieldhouse residence. There were six barns in this block up to about 1910.

1926 he bought a $300,000.00 bond issue on the Dixie Grande Hotel at Bradenton, Florida, and took every bond himself. He sold some afterwards, but later bought them back when the Hotel Operating Company failed to pay the interest and a year later he took the property over. The Hotel Company made him a deed, so he did not have to foreclose his mortgage. The 1926 storm, the same year the hotel was built, was what hurt Florida. He owned the hotel during his lifetime and his daughter Annetta Arbuckle still owns it.

One party to whom John sold $10,000.00 of these bonds was a woman who lived away from Elkhart. One day she took her coupons from the bonds into the bank where she lived, to deposit them. The banker told her that Florida was a flat tire, that if she bought bonds in Florida, she had made a very bad investment. After he told her that, she came to Elkhart on the first train. John told her he would redeem the bonds in a short time and gave her a writing to that effect. Later he took the bonds up and paid her the interest up to that date. Then she took the $10,000.00 to her banker, who had made fun of the Hotel Dixie Grande Bonds. She told him to invest it in what he thought would be good. He showed her a 5% issue on a large new building in a big city, and advised her to take all those bonds she could, as it was a good issue. She took $12,000.00 of those bonds and several years later lost the entire principal. It seemed the building was built on leased ground and during the 1933 depression the owner of the building neglected paying the annual rental, so the owner of the ground took the entire building, cancelling the 99 year lease. Things like that are what help to make life interesting.

John made another investment in Florida. It was at the time they were deepening the harbor at Miami to a 30 foot depth. The Clark Dredging Company had their contract nearly finished and they had borrowed about to the limit of their credit. P. C. Kendall was their Treasurer and he wired John to come to Florida. Kendall was a former Elkhart man, whom John knew well. John was in Boston at the time, attending a meeting of the National Real Estate Association, so after the convention, he took a bus to New York City and discovered the Clyde Line had a boat sailing for Miami the next day. So John boarded the boat, which took 3½ days. Kendall met him at the boat, took him to the dredges and showed him the small amount of work remaining, after which John made a loan to the Clark Dredging Company of $50,000.00. The loan was fully paid within six months, as the Company was paid in full as soon as their work was completed. John always liked to make a business trip and that trip gave him much pleasure. He met the President of the Southern Railroad on the boat and had a wonderful visit with him.

John always took much pleasure in doing something, and many a letter he wrote when he thought it would do some good. For instance, he wrote a well known furnace company once and told them that their furnace had the hardest grates to shake of any furnace on the market, because their grates were almost solid and were each 9 inches wide. He told them of another furnace that had narrow grates, and those grates were also hollow in the center and that furnace had the easiest grates to shake. They wrote him back, thanked him for the letter and stated the letter was sent to their engineering department. Two years later this same company was turning out grates $4\frac{1}{2}$ inches wide instead of 9, so that most any boy or woman could shake the ashes from the furnace, but with a 9 inch grate it took a strong man.

One day Emil Anderson, John's attorney, walked lame as he came into the office, for he had just fallen down the Elkhart Post Office steps. John took him home in his car and when he returned, he wrote a letter to the Post Office Department at Washington, D. C., and told them that a friend of his had just sprained his ankle on the Elkhart Post Office steps. He asked that, in building new Post Offices in the future why doesn't the government forget Roman architecture and get down to American architecture and build at least one Post Office so the stamp window is on the sidewalk level, the same as a modern up to date store room? He also stated that the New York City Post Office had 27 steps, before one got into the building. This was too much effort for thousands of people each day walking up those steps. The Architectural Department of Post Offices at Washington answered the letter and gave several reasons for the steps; that electric light bills were high throughout the nation and that basement rooms had to have daylight; that buildings would look squatty if built too low. John answered their letter by stating that rooms could be placed on the upper floor, giving far more light and ventilation and the building would not look squatty. He received a total of four letters from them and they seemed to be interested in his replies. John lived to see the day that stamp windows in some Post Offices were built on sidewalk level. He always thought that such letters did no harm, and he enjoyed writing them.

One day a store tenant phoned and wanted John to come to see the store. John went, and all he wanted to show him was the basement stairway, which was a nice stairway, but it had no handrail. The merchant stated that the insurance company with whom he insured his store help had written him that they had recently had 4 claims where people had fallen down basement stairways. Not one of those stairways had a handrail when these accidents had happened, so they were demanding that railings be placed on all stairways. John ordered the railing and thought it such a good idea, that he told his carpenter to place railings on all stairways, when he had the time. From that time on we noticed fewer reports of falls down stairways. Before that time, it seemed that each year someone would fall down a stairway and get badly hurt, perhaps breaking an arm or leg. There never was any question but that these railings prevented many a fall among nearly 400 tenants renting through the office.

One time John had a tenant who complained about neighborhood boys destroying his garden. It seemed that the boys next door invited many other boys to play ball in their yard and the ball would often go over the fence into our tenant's garden. On account of this he could never have a garden. His wife, however, would try to beat the boys to get the ball, and in a few months she had exactly 12 baseballs and one football which only helped the boys try to make life miserable for John's tenant, so John had the board fence torn down and erected a 4 foot new wire fence in its place. The wire fence was more difficult to climb, but the boys climbed it. The tenant even went to the police about it, but they could not do much about it.

After a time, he did not complain any more, so one day John asked him how the boys were behaving. The tenant remarked, "I have no trouble at all with the boys now, for I was telling my troubles to a New York Central Railway electrician and he said, "Tonight I will fix your fence for you." So after dark he came with full equipment. He first dug a small trench between fence and house and laid electric wires in it, which he attached to the house wiring, the other end of the wires he attached to the fence. By turning a switch, a coil would vibrate, and charge the fence with a low voltage and as long as the switch was on, the fence was charged with electricity. When his wife would happen to see the boys climbing the fence, she would turn the switch just about the time the boys were going over the top. The boys would immediately dance and get off of the fence as quickly as possible; they seemed bewildered. One day one of the boys brought his father to the fence and explained that at times it seemed to be charged. The father made this remark, after he touched the fence and felt the current, "Leave the fence alone, if it bothers you." This was good advice. All the boys thereafter avoided it and soon the electricity was left off all the time.

Soon afterwards John had another tenant who was complaining about neighbors. It seemed that a family with nine children moved in next door and the property they bought had no shade trees. As the house was one story, in the summer months it was very warm with the sun shining on the roof. John's property had a number of shade trees,

the back yard had six or seven and this entire family from next door spent much time
in summer under John's trees. The tenant
complained they were paying rent for the
back yard but could not use it, as the new
neighbors were using it. So John had a wire
fence erected around the whole back yard,
and ran the fence on both sides of the yard
clear to the street in front of the house. It
kept the older folks out, but not the children,
for they climbed the fence day after day to
get under the shade of the trees. The tenant
still complained, so John bought an electric
device for the fence, which immediately stopped the fence climbing.

Less than a week later the mother of the 9
children appeared at the office with a six year
old girl and she said, "Mr. Fieldhouse, do you
think it is right to put electricity through
small children?" John replied, "Yes in some
cases. You see, my tenants pay rent for the
back yard, but are unable to use it as much
as they would like to, on account of your
children occupying it most of the time. They
asked your children not to climb the fence,
but your children would not obey the orders.
Now, if your children don't touch that fence,
the electricity won't be on, but if they climb
the fence it will." The electricity was never
on after that, for the children quit climbing
the fence. Thereafter when tenants were
bothered by neighbors, John ordered fences
built. They always gave good results.

One time John had a house next to a family who owned their home and had five children, and John's tenant had three. After the tenant lived there for a year the children got to quarreling. This caused the mothers to quarrel, and later caused the husbands to fight. They were about an even match and after their fight, the owner put up a cable as near to the line as possible, supported by several posts. Then he said to John's tenant the next time he saw him, "Keep your children on the west side of the cable and I will keep mine on the east side; keep your wife on the west side and I will keep mine on the east side, and keep yourself on the west side and I will keep myself on the east side. Outside of that I have nothing more to say." For 1½ years there was no talking or visiting between the two separate families and neither paid any attention to the other. However, one day John went past the property and noticed the cable was gone, so when his tenant came in the office several weeks later to pay the rent, John asked, "What became of the cable?" To which the tenant replied, "Why, my neighbor to the east and his whole family were over to my house last Saturday night until 11 P.M., for we are now the best of friends." To which John replied, "Well how did that all happen so suddenly?" The tenant replied, "Well you see, John, my wife and I went to the Tabernacle Meeting one evening at the corner of Franklin and Fifth

Streets. After we sat down we beheld our neighbors several rows in front of us. It happened that the preacher, Rev. Lyon, spoke that evening on the subject of Neighbors. That night as we walked home, I told my wife and the children that hereafter we would speak to our neighbors. When I went to work the next morning I noticed the cable was gone, including the posts. Even the children spoke to our children the next time they saw them. We have all been the best of friends ever since." They lived side by side for many years thereafter and so far as we know, they never had any more trouble.

John never objected to renting to children, he said the more the merrier. At one time we had one family of 11 children, two of ten and two of eight. One time John rented a house to a man by the name of Hoffnadle, who was about the worst looking customer he ever had. He paid the first month's rent of $8.00, but never paid any more, and after eight months John had to set him out. Then the tenant moved to a house on Sycamore Street, next to a house that John owned. When he discovered that John owned that house next door, trouble began, for he made life disagreeable for John's tenants, so much so that they moved out. John rented the house three different times in six months, but each tenant stayed only one month. So John decided to leave the house vacant, which he did for a number of months. One day a man came in

John Fieldhouse in 1907, with Gyp & Topsy, a team he drove for 18 years and they never ran away.

and wanted to know what John had for rent, but we did not mention the house on Sycamore Street. The man finally remarked, "You have a house vacant on Sycamore Street." John said, "Yes, but I don't want to rent it as the next door tenant drives everybody out." To which the man replied, "I believe that I could live along side anybody without any trouble." John said, "If you think you can, the house rents for $8.00 but you will have to stay there 6 months if you take it." The man moved in and when he paid his second month's rent, we did not mention his neighbor, nor did we until the man paid the sixth month's rent. Then John asked him, "How do you get along with Hoffnadle?" The man replied, "Never had a better neighbor, we get along swell, although I believe we would have had trouble if you had not warned me. But just after we moved in, I went out in the back yard to hang up the clothes line, and over he came and said, "Do you know where the line is here?" I pointed to my ear and shook my head as if I could not hear, and he walked away. My wife went out later to hang up the clothes and over he came again and said to her, "Do you know where the line is here?" She shook her head and pointed to her ear and today yet he thinks we are both deaf and dumb. When anyone comes to the door, we always ask them in, so we get along fine."

Once John rented a house to a man and wife with no children and they lived there nearly a year without speaking to their neighbors. One night they drove home early, after a short automobile ride and they talked to their neighbor in the next yard for about half an hour, standing up all of the time. The next morning this neighbor called at the kitchen door, came in the house and visited for about 5 minutes. She repeated these calls each and every morning continuously, as long as the tenant lived there. As time went on she stayed longer. The tenant finally had to move in order to get rid of her morning calls, as the man's wife could not get her work done, because the neighbor often stayed as long as two hours. They did not want to make her mad, as she was nice in a way, but had two bad faults, calling too often and staying too long.

One time John had a large 9 room house, which was very close to the house next door, which made the rooms dark on the one side. The tenant who lived in the house for several years, came in the office quite excited one day, and said he was going to move, as the house was haunted. He said strange loud noises were heard in the house every night and, "They keep getting worse and before anything frightful happens we are going to move," and he did move that same day. He had told the whole neighborhood that the house was haunted. So John told the next tenant that the house was haunted, for he knew the neighbors would tell them, and he did not want them to move in if they were afraid. He eased their feelings somewhat however by telling them that he would give them one thousand dollars, if they would catch for him a ghost, to which they smiled, and moved in.

When they paid their next month's rent nothing was said about ghosts, but at the end of the year, John asked if they had been bothered by ghosts. The man replied, "Yes." He said they had been somewhat worried for several months by the strange noises, which almost at times made them feel sick with fright. One day, when he opened the basement door, as he turned on the light, he saw what he thought was a shadow pass across the basement floor. He made up his mind he was going to investigate and if possible find out the reason why this shadow appeared. After spending several hours, the mystery was solved, for he found 8 large bats in that basement. At night they would fly against the furnace hot air pipes, causing a strange noise that would make the people in the upper rooms tremble with fright.

John had one customer who was an old maid past 70 years of age. Up to that time she had never been alone overnight during her lifetime, as she had an old maid sister who lived with her. They were both very much afraid of ghosts and for that reason they always had plenty of light in the room at night. After the one sister died, she immediately got a 12 year old girl to come and live with her, with instructions never to leave her alone at night. The girl one night got so very sick that she was unable to get out of bed. At 1 A.M. there was a big flash of lightning and then the thunder roared, the wind slammed the stairway door with such a bang that this woman immediately realized that the upstairs windows were open, as the day before had been very warm. She said to the girl, "What will I do, what will I do? I have left the upstairs windows open, and the storm will rain in and wet the ceiling of our rooms below." The little girl, sick as she was, said, "Go up and shut the windows, same as you would in the daytime, for there is no one up there to hurt you. The rooms are just as vacant as they are in the daytime and I would gladly go and shut them if I was able to walk up the steps. I would not be the least bit afraid, for there is nothing up there to be afraid of." The woman thought to herself, as the storm was fast approaching, if that little girl is not afraid, why should I be? She immediately ascended the dark stairway, entered both rooms in the darkness, closed the windows and came down the stairway as slowly as she had gone up. After that she was never afraid for she lived alone in the same house for at least 8 years. She often remarked that her main regret was that she had partly ruined her life by always being afraid.

In the front office there is a basement door.

One day a woman with a boy about 5 years of age, entered the office and sat down with the boy to wait for the return of John Fieldhouse, whom I was expecting soon. But the woman waited nearly an hour before John came. During this time, the boy got uneasy and caused her some trouble taking care of him. She finally said to him, "If you don't behave, I will place you in this clothespress with a skeleton this man has in there. That skeleton will keep you quiet, for then if you don't behave, he will eat you up." The poor little fellow trembled with fear, and sat quiet as a mouse the balance of the time she was waiting. Such talk as that would affect that boy's life.

John's policy of renting to large families usually meant that we would have several families with ten or twelve children. Those families always stayed in one house a long time as it was usually difficult for them to get a house when the prospective landlord found out they had so many children. One woman once sent three of her children to a cemetery. When the landlord asked her if she had any children, she stated she had three in the cemetery. He rented her the house and he was very angry when he discovered she had three children living. She then reminded him that she had told him she had three children and they happened to be in the cemetery that certain afternoon.

The oldest tenant John had, originally had eleven children, and they rented the same house for more than forty-eight years. As a rule these tenants with large families were not hard on a house, as the children usually behaved. One of the eleven children of this certain family, a boy about 17 years old, wanted to hitchhike with another boy, who had T.B., to Arizona. After they got there he stayed with his boy friend for several years. Both drank out of the same tincup all of this time. When the boy returned home he had T.B. but did not know it. He drank out of the tincup at the kitchen sink, and a brother and sister also contracted T.B. All three have since died from T.B. The mother and two of her boys still rent of us.

One day a locomotive engineer came in the office with his wife and one boy about 7 years of age. John took them to see a $30.00 house he had vacant to see if he could rent it to them. When a house was vacant we usually pulled most of the window shades down to help keep the wall paper from fading. This boy made every shade roll to the top, and each time after he let the shade go, his father or mother would remark, "Don't do that." When they returned to the office, they decided to rent the house. But John said, "I have decided not to rent it to you, on account of the boy. He is a spoiled boy, for each time you told him not to roll the shade, he went to the next one and did it again, while you did nothing about it. That boy would be hard on the house, as you don't know how to control him." They took it alright, and admitted they were to blame. To our surprise, the man often called in the office afterwards and seemed just as friendly as he would have been if John had rented him the house. This was the only time that I ever remember John refusing to rent a dwelling house on account of a child.

It is a very interesting business, renting and selling houses, for one deals with all kinds of people. When they rent or buy a house in a certain location, the children grow up there. They get acquainted with other children in the same neighborhood and sometimes, later marry some boy or girl they grew up with. Sometimes a whole life is changed by taking a certain house in a certain district. For more than thirty years we have rented a skating rink in Elkhart, which used to be an Armory. The operator of this skating rink once told me that many people who get married meet each other for the first time at a skating rink and it has happened fully a dozen times at this local rink, while he has been operating it during a period of ten years.

The following, to me, is the most interesting story I have to offer. I still own the building, although my father owned it at the time. I have a proud feeling in owning a property where a wonderful discovery was made. In the year 1932 a man named C. J. Warnke came in the office, introduced himself as an inventor and wanted to rent a room for an experimental shop. John showed him a small building 20 by 30 feet at 515 Baldwin Street and rented it to him for $10.00 per month. He wanted window shades at all the windows, which John had installed for him. During his tenancy he only paid four months rent; then we did not see him for months. I stopped there a number of times, but he did not seem to be there. If he was there, he did not come to the door. That was during the depression and we were losing considerable rent, but as long as we had no special tenant for the building, we let it ride, until Charles Kraft, a pattern maker, inquired about renting the building. At this time, Warnke owed exactly $208.00. Kraft said he would take the room. So I went over and sawed the lock off, and with our truck moved two loads from the building, all the goods belonging to Warnke, and stored them in our warehouse out of the way in a far corner of the building. Charles Kraft moved in with his pattern shop. He is still there, but the building is four times larger than it used to be.

Four months after Kraft moved in, Warnke called at the office and asked where his personal property was. We told him we moved it to our warehouse, that we were not trying to hold it, and that he could get it anytime. Then he wondered if we would hold it longer, and we told him we would. He left it there nearly a year. One day he called for it, so I took him to the warehouse, showed him where it was, gave him the key and told him to return the key after he had his goods moved out, which he did. Nothing was said about the back rent, as we never expected to get it, and it was better to part friends than to be enemies.

Several years later this man Warnke called at the office one day and paid the $208.00 in currency. He said he had just come from the grocery store, where he had paid the groceryman $45.00 and the groceryman was amazed at the miracle, as he had long ago thought it was a no good account. Warnke told us that he would have starved, had it not been for this groceryman.

About two years later, Warnke again appeared at our office and made a friendly call, stayed and talked for about an hour. Just before he left, he asked, "Do you people know what I invented in the building I rented from you at 515 Baldwin Street?" We said, "No." He said, "These FLUORESCENT ELECTRIC LIGHTS that you now have in your office were invented by me, but improved by General Electric, as they bought the patent from me. I receive a very small royalty on each lamp manufactured and will for a 17 year period, but the royalty is so small that it will take me a very long time to get rich. General Electric was the only company I could go to, that was interested

Jackson Place, a part of Fieldhouse's Fourth Addition, where John built a total of 60 houses of this same type from 1895 to 1899, all modern with a few barns, but not one garage.

in my product, as I was without money and without friends."

Since that time, Warnke has called in this office a number of times, as he comes to Elkhart now and then. In my opinion his product paid him far more than he expected, as his lights are very popular throughout the U.S. and the world. Today he operates a factory in Chicago employing more than 400 people, but he spends most of his time in Colorado where he operates two mines. The American Magazine a number of years ago had an article stating that some man had invented FLUORESCENT LIGHTS and had sold out to General Electric, and mentioned the fact that the light was almost perfect. Railroad trains use them today and there is hardly a store or office without them.

In one of John's houses there was a clothespress door with a door-knob on the outside only. The square shaft through the door, operating the door catch only extended half an inch inside the clothespress. There was a carpet on the floor and the housewife had discovered moths in the carpet. She was saturating the carpet with formaldehyde solution to kill the moths. The fumes were strong in the small clothespress, and as she was inside, the door accidentally shut as she leaned against it. When she tried to open it she found no knob, but only the very small shaft. By this time she was beginning to choke and gasp for breath from the strong fumes. She had to think quickly what to do, as there was no one else in the house. She took off her apron, and wound the strings around the small, square shaft. After it was in a ball about one inch in diameter she frantically opened the door, and immediately fainted away in the hallway. She came about as close to death as one could and then escape, for if she had not acted quickly, or not had an apron on, she would have fainted in the clothes-press and would have been found dead. Such items as loose door knobs are seldom thought of, but in building it is well to have everything as safe as possible, for a large percentage of accidents happen in the home.

John had two tenants during his career whose deaths were caused by filling a gasoline stove while the burner was lighted. The gasoline overflowed onto the flame and set the houses on fire. John had another tenant who had an oil burning heating stove, which accidentally sprang a leak and caught on fire. The tenant could have let the house burn down, but he lifted the stove and carried it outdoors while the fire was burning. He was badly burned trying to save the house, for within a few days he died. One tenant was dressing her two year old child, close to a wood stove, which was burning with the door open. Unknown to her, the back of her dress touched the flame from the burning wood. The back of her dress was on fire and as she ran for help to a neighbor's home 400 feet away, she fell exhausted and died. The child was still sitting in the highchair unhurt.

Years ago, when John built a house he also built a cistern, which was usually placed under a back porch. One time years later some girls about six years old were playing in the back yard and one of them crawled under the back porch. The cistern cover boards were badly rotted, which broke with her weight and allowed her to fall into a well filled cistern and she was drowned. It was tragedy for that family. There were several such cistern accidents, one where a woman had a trap door in the pantry, with the cistern below. She took up the trap door to get a bucket of water. She forgot to close the trap door and later she accidently walked into the opening and drowned in the cistern. After that John had all his cisterns filled with dirt, as he considered them a hazard. Also a number of rock gardens in which children were accidently drowned, where the water was deep.

That has been the purpose of this book, to give a little experience along the realestate line, as one who ventures into it has much to learn and while this book does not cover many points, it gives a few experiences of one who liked the work of building homes for people to live in and it was most interesting to see these homes occupied as years went past and watch the families who occupied them grow. As the old saying reads, and it is a true one, "There is no place like home."

When a man and his wife own their home they are usually good citizens. The people who do not own their own homes, miss some of the pleasures of life. So while we live, let us live in a home, all our own. It is one form of life insurance. The older one gets, the faster time flies.

John W. Fieldhouse died June 21, 1938, at 7:15 P.M., the longest day of the year, age 87. His wife Mary J. Fieldhouse, died March 9, 1945, at 10:30 P.M., age 93. Inheritance tax on both estates were paid within one year from the date of their deaths. The inheritance tax rate today is much higher than it was then, which is one reason that I have not tried to make too much money. On my own dwelling house properties during the past 12 years I have not raised one rent, unless the tenant wanted some improvements. However in these houses I have done nothing in the line of decoration, which I let the tenant take care of. If I get a house vacant in poor condition, I have no trouble renting it and the tenant will take it as is and fix it up, if I rent it at the same price. Today my highest priced house is $40.00, my lowest priced house is $7.00.

This $7.00 tenant has rented of this office over 30 years. Two years ago she came in with a total of 6 months rent at $14.00 per month and said to me, "Charlie, everyone asks me how much rent I pay and I am ashamed to tell them. Here is six months rent at $14.00 per month. Give me a receipt so I can tell them what I am paying." I wrote her a receipt for one year in advance. She did not notice it until she got home, and then she phoned me. The next year she came in with twelve dollars and said make it for one month. I gave her a receipt for seven dollars plus a five dollar bill. Then she said, "Charlie, why are you so bull headed?" I told her, "I have told 2792 people that I have not raised a dwelling house tenant in 12 years, which is unusual these high priced times. Now if I would raise your rent, I could not tell that any more, and I get quite a kick out of telling that story."

In the horse and buggy days, John had one bad runaway with a team of horses. I was with him and another man. The center pole dropped between the two horses, as he was driving over a ditch. This caused the buggy to go against both horses, which scared them and they ran away. The other man and I were thrown out of the single seated buggy, and my father went over the dash, holding onto the lines. He and the team went through an old barb wire fence and John was badly cut on the face, just below one eye, which left a mark he carried for life. The team was covered with blood when we found them at the barn door in the alley, after a teamster had brought us home in a dirt wagon. This was the second time John had a runaway with this team, so he sold them within a week and bought Gyp and Topsy, each 3 years old. He drove them for 18 years. He could trust them to stand anywhere. Gyp and Topsy never ran away. They were a perfect team and we kept them in a barn back of the house where we lived, with two buggies and a cutter.

At that time there were 6 barns on the two alleys in our square block and automobiles had not been thought of. Runaways were quite numerous. At that time Elkhart had a horse drawn street car with no conductor. The cars were short and the driver of the one horse could hear the 5 cent pieces ring four bells as the nickel or pennies would fall against them after being put in the slot of a glass front box. It would take about 5 seconds before the change hit the bottom of the container. The horse was changed on these street cars about every three hours as they passed the car barn. In the horse and buggy days there was no paving to speak of. Mr. Hugg, paid monthly by some people, operated for many years a sprinkler wagon to lay the dust on certain streets, near the center of Elkhart.

When I was 9 years old, my mother bought for me a little seven dollar theatre about 18 inches square at Marshall Field's in Chicago. It had sets of scenery, a city scene, a woods scene and a room scene. With it were paste board figures of men and women, with strings attached at the bottom, which could be pulled, and the figures would cross the stage in the sawed groove in the floor board. There were drop curtains, which rolled up and down by pulling strings. When Ervin Nadel, a boy my same age, who lived a block away saw it, he came down every night to play with that theatre in our basement, until his folks bought him one like it a month later. In my opinion Ervin Nadel's life was influenced by those two miniature theatres. He traveled throughout the United States in vaudeville for 8 years, after which he located in New York City, where he still lives. For many years he looked over vaudeville talent and told them what his company would pay for their act. My little theatre was stolen from my workbench in the basement of our house, together with my miniature train, about 15 years after my mother bought them for me. This was a big disappointment to me. They don't make miniature theatres and trains today like those were made.

In the days before fumigating, John had an old house that was just alive with bed bugs. He let a certain woman who was extra good at cleaning, have the house three months for nothing, thinking she might get rid of them. She moved out before three weeks because she could not cope with the situation. John then rented the house at half price on account of the bugs and the tenant lived in the house for a number of years, but said nothing about the bugs. When he did finally move, John asked him if the bedbugs were still there. He said, "There have never been any bugs in the house after the first week I lived there. When we moved in we decided to move right out. But I happened to think that if anything would kill them, it would be Elkhart gas, as I worked at the gas plant. So I borrowed a street key from the gas company, turned on the gas jets, and locked the doors and windows. In one hour we turned off the gas in the street with the key. Twenty four hours later when we visited the house, there were no live bedbugs, but plenty of dead ones."

In one way it was a dangerous experiment. Later on we had a house vacated at 149 E. Marion Street in the center of Elkhart. The new tenant moved in late one afternoon. He connected up his gas stove, so his wife could cook supper, by which time it was dark. When he turned on the gas meter they soon discovered a gas leak. The smell was rather strong in the front room and he noticed it was much stronger on the front stairway. So he went to the kitchen for a lighted oil lamp. His wife and daughter followed him up the stairway. When they reached the room upstairs there was a grand explosion, throwing the front wall of the house out into the street. All three were taken to the hospital, where they remained for several weeks. The former tenant had a gas stove upstairs and when he moved he disconnected it, leaving the gas pipe open.

About the year 1890, Ferdinand August Buescher was working for C. G. Conn in his band instruument factory. A few years later he quit his job with Conn and started a factory of his own, which gradually grew year by year until about 1903 he employed more than 100 men and women, manufacturing different kinds of band instruments. About that year the Indiana National Bank failed and, as the factory owed that bank, it was almost impossible for the factory to borrow money elsewhere. So the Buescher Manufacturing Company, then located in a two story building at the southeast corner of North Main and Simonton Streets was forced to go into bankruptcy, which left F. A. Buescher without any money on hand whatever.

Early in the spring of 1904 F. A. Buescher happened to come in the office, while Mr. Fieldhouse was talking with Charles L. Monger, owner of the Monger Office Building. Just after Mr. Buescher came in, John W. Fieldhouse said to Charles Monger, "Charles if you will loan August Buescher $2,000.00 on his personal note to start him up in the band instrument business again, I will do the same." Charles Monger said at once, "I will," August Buescher immediately looked for a building to start a factory, but could find no suitable building, so John W.

Fieldhouse residence.

Fieldhouse asked him what kind of building he wanted. Buescher said that he wanted a two story brick building 40 by 80 feet and he made the remark that that was as big as he would ever want, as he did not care to work more than 20 people.

So Mr. Fieldhouse built him the building at number 225 East Jackson Street, Elkhart, Indiana, and Mr. Buescher started operations there October 15, 1904. Mr. Buescher rented this building at $40.00 per month until the fore part of 1909 at which time F. A. Buescher and John H. Collins, his partner and friend, wanted the building enlarged, which Mr. Fieldhouse did, charging them $120.00 per month from June 1, 1909.

June 1, 1914, the Buescher Band Instrument Company bought the land and building they had been renting. The company kept on buying additional ground and enlarging, and worked as high as 300 to 400 people, while Buescher was with the company, the man who said in 1904 that he would never work more than 20 people. But this was not all. At about the time August Buescher moved into his new factory in 1904, there was a musician who lived in Elkhart by the name of Edward LeFevre who was known as the greatest saxaphone player in the world. At that time neither LeFevre nor any one else could get all the notes in playing a saxaphone. When playing with a band, it did not always make so much difference, as the other instruments would fill in the gap of missed notes. But a saxaphone solo was not too nice to listen to, as many notes were missed, and it was almost impossible to run the scale and get every note perfect, for they would be off tune a little or not sound at all. August Buescher was the only man who perfected and made a perfect saxaphone. He worked on the problem hour after hour and finally made one that was so good that every note could be heard perfectly.

But it was not long until most all other band instrument factories were also making perfect saxaphones, for in obtaining one of Buescher's Saxaphones, all they had to do was to saw the Buescher Saxaphone in two, pound both sides flat and they had the Buescher pattern. Although Buescher and Collins with other stockholders afterwards sold out to other interests who are still operating the Buescher plant, and F. A. Buescher and J. H. Collins have since died, the Buescher name will long live in music circles, for each saxaphone made today has a history behind it pertaining to August Buescher.

About fifty years ago some Elkhart citizens decided to build a new hospital, as the one we had then was far from perfect. One day Dr. J. C. Fleming, Herman Borneman and Conrad Ziesel called at John's office and asked him where to build the new hospital. John told them that he knew a good place. He could not explain it, but he could show them

the only place for it, if they would get into
his double seated buggy, which was in front
of the office. They wanted to know without
going, as Dr. Fleming said he should be at
his office. John told them he would have
them back in half an hour, so they finally
went. John took them to the edge of Mc-
Naughton Park on a high bank, where a nice
view of the beautiful St. Joseph River would
be seen from the front of the hospital, if
built there. They all agreed it was a perfect
spot and told John to find out what the six
large lots and one house could be bought for.
John had the answer in three days and the
Elkhart General Hospital was built there and
has been enlarged several times since. If
John had told them of the spot they probably
would not have been interested.

Hub Beardsley of Elkhart at one time was
a heavy stockholder in Hotel Elkhart and
they were building a large addition to the
hotel of about 100 rooms. John was not a
stockholder, as he owned the Hotel Bucklen.
The Hotel Elkhart would need more park-
ing room, so Hub Beardsley asked Mr. and
Mrs. Withers what they would take for their
8 room house and lot just back of Hotel Elkhart. Their price was $15,000.00. Six years
before John Fieldhouse had sold the same
property to a Mr. and Mrs. Jeffrey for
$4,200.00 who several years later sold to Mr.
and Mrs. Withers. Hub offered Mr. and Mrs.
Withers $8,000.00 for their property; a week

later he offered $9,000.00, later $10,000.00, then $11,000.00 and finally $12,000.00, after which Hub Beardsley came to John Fieldhouse and said, "The Hotel Elkhart will have to pay Mr. and Mrs. Withers $15,000.00 for their property." John said, "It can be bought for less than that." Hub said, "No, it cannot, for they know we have to have it for parking room." John said, "Hub will you give $12,-000.00 for it?" Hub said, "Yes." John said, "Then you have just bought it, for I can deliver it to you within a week for $12,000.00 and could have bought it for far less than that if you had come to me in the first place. All I ask of you, Hub, is to keep away from Mr. and Mrs. Withers for one week. If you do so, I will deliver the deed to you in less than a week for $12,000.00." Hub said, "I bet you cannot buy it a dollar less than $15,000.-00." John said in a joking way, "Hub, you know how to make and sell patent medicine, but you don't know anything about buying real estate, otherwise you would have come to me in the first place."

That evening John went down to see Mr. and Mrs. Withers. They were at home, so John asked them if they would care to take an automobile ride. Mrs. Withers said, "No, we will not sell this property, Mr. Fieldhouse, for less than $15,000.00." John said, "I asked you both if you would take a ride with me." And again she said, "No." So John sat down and talked with them for half an hour about other things and she finally said, "Mr. Fieldhouse, we will take a ride with you, because I just want to see what you are up to." By this time it was dark, but that made no difference, so John started out with them, and drove 8 blocks to a 9 room vacant dwelling centrally located, a corner property on two paved streets. This house he had bought three months before, the former Conrad Ziesel home, from an Elkhart merchant, who had built a new brick home on Riverside Drive.

John had placed the house in perfect condition, with new hard wood floors, all newly varnished, clear across each room, except the kitchen, which had new linoleum. The house had just been remodeled throughout, with white enamel woodwork, new electric light fixtures, with lights all ready to turn on. Windows had been washed inside and out, and had new window shades, too. The water was on, so when the faucets were turned, water came, an important thing in selling a house, as they could see the plumbing was in good shape. He also had a new floor installed in the attic and also electric lights. John spent one hour showing them the house from attic to basement, and when they finally came to the front door, John made this remark, "Hub Beardsley told me today that he had offered you people $12,000.00 for your East Marion Street property. Well, I have just one story, and I don't want your answer until

9 o'clock tomorrow morning. Hub Beardsley and I joke a good deal and if your answer is "No," the joke is on me. If your answer is "Yes," the joke is on Hub. Hub told me today that you wanted $15,000.00 for your property and he had offered you $12,000.00. Now I ask $10,000.00 for this Ziesel home, placed in perfect condition. If you want to accept Hub's offer of $12,000.00, I will deed you this property and give you the $2,000.00 in currency. Now, I don't have to explain to you that this is a better house than yours, or that you can get better roomers here than you can in your run down house on East Marion Street, for you know that without my telling you. Just think it over until I call you in the morning for your answer."

Promptly at 9 the next morning, John made the call and got his answer "Yes." I went down for their abstract and got it brought to date by one absract company, took my father's abstract to the other abstract company and had his brought to date. Just 4 days and 2 hours from the time Hub Beardsley was in father's office, John walked into Hub Beardsley's office and said to him, "Hub, here is the deed made out to you for the Withers' property, and here is Emil Anderson's opinion as attorney, which shows a good title, so give me your check, Hub, for $12,000.00 as you agreed." Hub was amazed and bewildered and remarked as he was making out the check, "How do you do it, John?"

John replied, "It's easy, Hub, when one knows how." Hub Beardsley, so far as we know, never knew how it was done, but everyone was happy.

John W. Fieldhouse made similar deals more than once. When someone did not want to sell their property, he would look around and tempt them, by trading them a better home than they had. He often bought a run down property at low price, and revamped it in good condition, before he showed it. If the trade did not work out, he would hold it vacant, as stock on hand to sell. Usually it would not be very long until he would have it sold on contract to someone who would come in and inquire for a home or rental house. If John ever wanted to sell a property, he would always inquire next door to see if the adjoining owner was interested. Quite often they were. Once he tried the people next door on both sides, but neither was interested. He did not think of the man in back on the other street. That man several months later came in to inquire about the property and bought it.

One time in the horse and buggy days, a farmer 5 miles north of Elkhart, who was fairly well off, came in the office and said to John, "I came away from home and forgot my pocket book. Give me $10.00 and I will return it next time I come to town." John advanced him the amount, which was the first time, and when that farmer died about 15 years later, John had six small loan notes against him, which amounts John got from the farmer's administrator, all on account of that first loan. All down through the years we had many calls from people wanting small or large loans. John often made loans, but turned down 75% of the calls. The office still has many small notes that were never paid. He often told different people, if they wanted to go into business, where he would send them lots of customers, to go into the money loaning business.

In the year 1914 my father and mother and I were on an auto trip to Chicago. Near Rolling Prairie we had a flat tire and we stopped to change tires at the end of a sidewalk leading to a farm house. Before we got away, a woman from the farm house came out to sweep off the sidewalk. As she got to within ten feet of our car, she asked, "Tire trouble?" My father said, "Yes." She said, "Where are you going?" Father said, "To Chicago." Then she said, "Where did you come from this morning?" John said, "Elkhart." Then she said, "I know a man in Elkhart." John asked, "Who?" She said, "John Fieldhouse." John said, "Do I look like John Fieldhouse?" She said, "Are you John Fieldhouse?" He said, "That is what they call me in Elkhart." It happened that they both went to White Pigeon school at the same time and they had not seen each other in over forty years. We brought her a large box of candy on our return trip, and saw her several times later but she finally moved elsewhere.

One time a man named Pletcher Chase whom John had not seen since he attended school at White Pigeon, forty years before, called at the office. When Pletcher Chase asked me where John Fieldhouse was, I sent him to Benham's Livery Stable, one block away. As soon as he asked for John Fieldhouse, John immediately said, "Hello, Pletcher Chase." John would not have known him, but he knew his voice, and he had not seen him in over forty years.

The above reminds me of three stories that my father repeated many times, and all were very interesting to me.

In the fore part of October, 1880, Lottie Davis, 19 years old, came to Elkhart to stay all night with John and Mary Fieldhouse, so she could buy a dress at an Elkhart store, as she was going to marry Rev. Farrell Hart, also of White Pigeon. She told Mrs. Field-house that they were going to Grand Haven, Michigan, on their wedding trip to visit her husband's relatives, and from there they were going to cross Lake Michigan on the "Al-pena" for Milwaukee and that she dreaded that part of the trip as she was afraid of water. At Milwaukee they were going to visit some more of her husband's relatives. Then from there they were to go to Chicago, then back home. On the evening of October 16, 1880, they boarded the Alpena at Grand

John W. Fieldhouse about 1910.

Haven. It was a wild night, as there was lightning in the west, and it was very windy. She wanted her husband to cancel the boat trip, according to the relatives who came down to the boat to see them off, but he said, "This boat has seen many other storms before and always weathered them," so they went on the boat. The boat left at 9 o'clock for Milwaukee, but it never made port. The "Alpena" went down with all on board somewhere in Lake Michigan.

About the year 1860, a young man named Chancey Barnes, who lived on a farm with his parents, near White Pigeon, one afternoon at recess asked a school teacher at Stone Lake school to go to a dance with him at White Pigeon that evening. She refused to go with him to the dance, as she told him that she did not care to go with him anymore, as she was going with another young man. Then he pulled out a revolver, shot her twice and instantly killed her. He then shot himself in the head 4 times, shot one eye out, but still lived. Two hours later the Sheriff came. After his trial, he was sent to the penitentiary at Michigan City for a life term. He was found to be a model prisoner, so in 20 years he was pardoned and released from prison. He went back to White Pigeon and remained there for ten days. He was not treated very well by some people who remembered about the school teacher. So on the eleventh day he returned to the Michigan City prison and told the warden, "I was sent here for life, lock me up again and let me serve my full term." The warden did, and Chancy Barnes' grave is just west of the prison wall.

About 1865, a boy named Ivason Whyland had a revolver, whose trigger he snapped several times while on a walk with Frank Timmis and John Fieldhouse one Sunday afternoon. As they were walking through a woods, the three boys met Ellen Fieldhouse and another girl about her same age, who were also taking a Sunday afternoon walk. When the boys and girls were about 100 feet apart, Ivason Whyland pointed the revolver at the two girls, who were walking arm in arm, and said, "Couldn't I shoot them though?" As he made that remark, he pulled the trigger, the revolver went off, and the bullet went between the girls heads, as they plainly heard it whistle past. The boy was so scared he turned perfectly white and fainted away. It was a very close call for both of the girls.

In going into vacant houses, I always shut the door when I enter, as twice, in entering houses and leaving the door open, a cat has walked in, unnoticed. Several weeks later, on entering the same houses, I found dead cats, which were imprisoned and died from starvation. Once a family moved out of a house and left a family cat inside. When I entered the house several weeks later, I found the dead cat curled up on the kitchen register.

That was about 25 years ago. Every time I pass that house I remember that poor cat.

An Elkhart man by the name of Colonel Charles Girard Conn came back from the Civil War, having been a prisoner at Libbey Prison during the latter part of the war. Col. Conn organized a 12 piece band, as he knew how to play a cornet. One holiday, his band was parading down Main Street in Elkhart. A farm boy rode through the band, in the opposite direction on horseback. Conn hollared to him, "Don't do that again." As the boy tried it again, Conn handed his cornet to a fellow bandsman, then pulled the young man from his horse and a street fight ensued. Conn got the worst of the fight, as he was hit in the mouth, causing his lip to bleed badly. Conn paid no special attention to it, as he was a little drunk at the time. When the lip finally healed there was a notch in it, which greatly bothered Conn afterwards in playing his cornet. At that time, about 1872, a cornet mouthpiece went in the mouth like a cigar. Conn obtained a block of hard rubber, carved it out so it would go over the mouthpiece of his cornet. The other end fitted over the lips like a small cup. Nearly every horn player who saw it, wanted Conn to make one for him, too, which gave Conn the idea of making them to sell. So Conn rented an upstairs room next door to the Fieldhouse meat market, secured a second hand sewing machine, turned it into a lathe, and for two years he spun out rubber mouth pieces and sold them as fast as he could make them.

One day a Frenchman called on Conn, asked if he could use his workbench to repair some horns he had with him. Conn said, "Help yourself, and stay as long as you want." The Frenchman stayed two weeks. Conn stopped his work, and watched the Frenchman work repairing the horns. By the end of two weeks, Conn knew how to make a horn.

Conn made his first cornet in 1875. He hired another man to help him and began the manufacture of band instruments. He soon outgrew his upstairs quarters, and moved to a shop on ground level, less than a block away. Soon he outgrew this building, so built a larger factory. Today Elkhart has 22 band instrument factories, counting large and small ones and today C. G. Conn, Ltd., is the largest band instrument factory in the world, all on account of a street fight.

In some ways Col. Conn was a wonder. For 25 years Conn was also the editor and owner of the Elkhart Truth, a daily newspaper and he wrote an editorial for the paper each day. He at one time was a Congressman in Washington, and there, for awhile, he owned and edited a newspaper. However, at times, Conn was a heavy drinker. At one time, while drunk, he rode into the Hotel Bucklen Bar Room on horseback and with a revolver shot off and broke whiskey and beer bottles from the bar. He broke the large mirrors of the bar and even shot through the plate glass window of the barroom on Main Street as he rode out of the front door. The next day, however, Conn paid for the total damage, while he laughed about his folly. This act advertised him far and wide.

Conn was getting worse with the drink habit and one day while he was serving in Congress, he took a train for New York City on a business trip. After the train had left Washington, Conn was sitting in a seat of the day coach, next to the window, with a stranger. As the train sped along, Conn took a whiskey flask from his inside coat pocket, took the cork out and asked the stranger if he would have a drink. The stranger refused. Then Conn took several swallows, replaced the cork and returned the flask to his inside pocket, while the train rolled on. Half an hour later the stranger remarked, "I don't know who you are, but when the train arrived in Washington, I noticed you walking up and down the station platform a number of times, and thought you were about the nicest looking man that I had ever seen." Conn did walk straight, like a soldier. He was 6 feet 2 inches in height, and his hair was always long, which made him look like a musician. The stranger added, "But when I saw you take that whiskey flask from your pocket and drink from it, you went down 80% in my opinion, as I have no faith in a man who drinks whiskey. What good does that whiskey ever do you? No one can ever depend on you, as you are liable to be drunk at any time. When you are needed for any important work, you may be drunk." Conn knew the man was telling the truth. Before the train reached New York, Conn shook hands with this stranger and said, "I have enjoyed your wonderful talk and I am going to make you a promise that I will always keep. Never again in my lifetime will I ever taste strong drink." Conn then raised the car window, emptied the contents of the flask on the ground, then let the expensive flask fall to the ground, as the train sped on. Never again in Conn's lifetime did he touch strong drink, not even beer.

Conn was well off financially. He went to Europe, bought a large yacht, hired seven men to run it across the Atlantic Ocean, and through the Great Lakes to St. Joseph, Michigan, where he kept it for several years. Conn had a daughter named Sally and she asked my two sisters to take a week's trip on this yacht on Lake Michigan two different years with a number of other girls, who were Sally's friends, too. During Conn's lifetime, he had a number of yachts, having two at one time on the California coast.

Conn at one time bought a large portion of Elkhart Hydraulic stock, which included a large dam across the St. Joseph River at Elkhart with a number of raceways where

different factories used waterpower for manufacturing. In addition there was a steam
generating plant, which made electricity,
when water in the river was low, as the company furnished electricity to dwellings, stores
and factories in the city of Elkhart. There
was a competitor, the Indiana & Michigan
Electric Company, who got their current
from other dams and power houses along the
St. Joseph River. There was rivalry between
the two companies. Each advertised heavily
in the local newspapers, the Elkhart Review
and the Elkhart Truth. The I & M was a
little too much for the Elkhart Hydraulic
Company. One night the raceway to the
water power plant washed out where the dirt
bank was not high enough. This caused all
plants to shut down. Elkhart Hydraulic customers were out of light and power, until the
bank was replaced by sand bags and fill dirt,
which took time and money. Conn had other
bad luck at the time, as he was deep in debt.
In installing new dynamos, water wheels
and power lines throughout the city, his expenses were more than he had realized, and
after the raceway washed out his creditors
began asking him for money, which he did
not have. The banks were not willing to loan
him more, as they realized he was in bad
shape, although he had spent much money in
improving the hydraulics.

About this time he called on John Fieldhouse for advice. John said to Conn, "I un-

derstand you have $100,000.00 worth of paintings throughout your large residence. Would you be willing to include them in a bond issue covering everything you own?" Conn said, "Yes." "Then give me a list of all the items you owe." Conn brought the list in the folowing day and it totaled $140,000.00. John took it upon himself to sell a bond issue for Conn. While the bond issue papers were being made, which took several weeks, John went to Conn's largest creditors and influenced them to sign up for bonds. They refused at first, but when John told them if Conn went into the hands of a receiver, they would not get 25 cents on the dollar, where if they took 6% bonds due in five years, they would get 100 cents, most all of them signed. John got H. E. Bucklen to take $20,000.00 of the bonds, and a man named Mitch Charnley of Goshen, Indiana, who had a lot of confidence in Conn, took $40,000.00 of the bonds, as an investment. John took $30,000.00 and every bond was disposed of.

Charles G. Conn then went to work in earnest. He was at the factory at 6 A.M. every morning from then on, and stayed at the factory until 10 P.M. each night. The first morning he fired several employees for being late to work, and he walked up and down the aisles all day long. When he saw a man was not busy working, he called him down. One man, who worked for Conn at the time, told John that he used to spin out 75 keys a day,

but when Conn fired several men for not
working fast enough, that man turned out
almost double that number of keys, so Conn
would not call him down, or discharge him.

After the bonds were all taken, John said to
Conn, "Get rid of the hydraulics, for it is out
of your line. Your work is making band instruments and not furnishing electric current,
with a competitor in the same territory, Conn
gave John the agency and John tried to sell
the hydraulics to H. E. Bucklen, as Bucklen
then owned the Elkhart Water Works, and
John told him he could use the water power
for pumping water by electric current. John
had the deal almost closed for $225,000.00,
but a man named Ferber, an enemy of Conn's,
happened to ride on the train with Bucklen
to Chicago, and he told Bucklen that the
water power was nothing but trouble, that
it almost busted Conn and it might bust him.

John then went to his next prospect, the
Indiana & Michigan Electric Co. He immediately saw they were anxious for it, so the
deal was made within a short time, and the
bond issue was paid in full, long before the
due date, as Conn made money when he put
in the long hours in his factory. The Indiana & Michigan Electric Company bought
overflow rights, built a new dam in front of
the old dam and, with the other dams, plus
the Hen Island steam plant, they were in
good shape to furnish all the electric power
needed for the whole surrounding territory.

Mary J. Fieldhouse about 1910.

The old raceways in time were filled in and used as industrial sites.

Col. Conn however was on easy street again. He bought another yacht on the Pacific Coast and made his headquarters at Catalina Island, where he spent about half his time. He kept manufacturing horns much faster than he could sell them, as he was expecting a strike and had in storage fully $140,000.00 worth of manufactured goods ahead, when one night at about two o'clock in the morning, his four story red brick factory burned to the ground, burning to death two watchmen. He only had a total of $80,000.00 fire insurance. Conn was in California at the time. Some people thought, including ourselves, that it was one of his enemies who burned it, as Conn had a few, largely on account of his newspaper, as he was great in going after certain people at times.

This fire was a great blow to Conn, but he came back and was figuring on buying the Gossard Corset Factory building, on Sterling Avenue, in the south part of Elkhart. When John heard about Conn buying this plant, he immediately got in touch with him and said, "Conn, why don't you build a new factory, just as you want it, on the west part of your 240 acre farm, which part lies inside the City of Elkhart? It will help to increase the value of your farm." Conn worked at that time between three and four hundred people. He caught the idea and within one week he was throwing dirt for his new factory. At the same time the Angledile Scale Company wanted a new factory built, so Conn agreed to build them a factory also on a part of his farm, adjoining the Conn plant. As both buildings neared completion, Conn was again very hard up. As he had bought new machinery, he found his total indebtedness was nearing $250,000.00 so again he called on John Fieldhouse for help. Again he mortgaged his paintings, both factory buildings, his farm, his residence and everything he had. Charnley took $50,000.00 of the bonds. The total issue was $240,000.00. With hard work by John, the 7% bonds were all disposed of and later paid by Conn. In a short time Conn sold his Elkhart interests to Carl Greenleaf for $400,000.00 and Col. Charles Girard Conn went back to California. He lived to the age of 87. He was buried in Grace Lawn Cemetery in Elkhart, and has a nice monument with a cornet carved on the stone near the top.

At one time Col. Conn got very mad at a man named Marion Proctor and Conn spent much time talking about Proctor. One day Proctor called at the Conn factory to see Conn. Conn welcomed him with open arms, took Proctor through the new factory and explained all operations to him. After which he took him to his private office, offered Proctor a cigar and visited with him for half an hour. As they came into the main office again, Conn said to Proctor, "Marion, how did you come over, did you walk?" Marion said, "Yes." Conn then said, "Mr. Carnes, take Mr. Proctor in my car to any place he wants to go." As Proctor and Carnes left, William J. Gronert, Conn's office manager, said to Conn, "I have heard you call Marion Proctor all kinds of names. You said that you were going to get even with him and here you entertain him as if he were a king." To which Conn replied, "Well, if you are going to swat a man, you don't want to let him know you are mad at him, do you?"

Col. Conn never evened up with Marion Proctor for the grudge he had against him, but Marion Proctor had his share of grief, which in a way was the cause of his death. He lost his only child, a daughter, when she was 26 years old. His wife died within six months from the time the daughter died, which left Marion Proctor alone in the world. He however was a rich man and went to live in a warmer climate in the State of Mississippi, where he bought a 20 acre Pecan Grove, with no buildings. He lived at a local hotel. Proctor always wore a silk plug hat, which made him distinguished looking. One Sunday he told two traveling men that he owned $15,000.00 in U.S. Bonds. The traveling men refused to believe him, so on Monday Proctor went to the bank, got the bonds from his bank box, took the men to his room and showed them the fifteen $1,000.00 bonds. The men were surprised and talked with Proctor in his room for several hours about different things, after which Proctor took his newspaper package back to the bank lockbox. Four months later, Proctor went to the bank to clip his coupons, only to find a newspaper bundle containing no bonds, in his box. The two men had in someway stolen his $15,000.00 U.S. unregistered bonds. Proctor died from worry within a few months, as the bonds were never recovered.

Proctor years before owned 82½ feet square, across the street from my father's new residence, built in 1892. Before the house was two years old Proctor had an item in the local paper that he was going to build a new brick livery stable building on his vacant lot for liveryman Ross Bowles, who had an old frame livery stable one block away. Proctor evidently thought that father would buy the lot to keep the livery stable from being built. Proctor hired an architect to make plans and again mentioned that fact in the paper. Father thought there was something to it, but as he sat on his front porch one evening, Ross Bowles went past driving a hack. Ross never even looked at the lot as he drove past, which plainly showed father there was no livery stable to be built for Ross Bowles, for, if so, he would have looked at the lot as he drove past. One day Proctor came in John's office and showed him the livery stable plans, with horses in the basement, rigs on the main floor and hay, corn and oats in the loft. He told John that $10,000.00 would buy the lot, otherwise the livery stable would immediately be built. Proctor's plan did not work, as John told him that if a livery stable were built it would be just the place for John to keep Gyp and Topsy, his buggy team, and that he would like to see Bowles have a nice brick livery stable on that spot. Proctor went out discouraged. His little trick did not work. Years later, in 1916, he sold the lot to the Christian Science Church, who built a nice church on it.

I had a cousin, John Sandhovel, who had always lived in South Bend, where he worked for the South Bend Watch Company. After his father died, about 1919, his mother, sister and he moved to Los Angeles, California, where his mother bought a small house from funds she received from the sale of the South Bend home. For three years John Sandhovel could find no work. It seemed to him there were three men for each job. However, one day he was walking for the first time down a railroad track. He noticed a building that looked like a factory, so he climbed a fence, went to the office, asked the manager for work, and as usual was turned down. He walked several hundred feet away when it suddenly began to rain, so he ran back to the office for shelter. While there the manager asked him what part of the country he was from. Sandhovel replied, "South Bend, Indiana." The manager asked. "What did you do there?" John replied, "Watchmaker for the South Bend Watch Company." The manager said, "Are you a watchmaker? If so, we could use you, as this is a movie camera lens factory." John worked for that factory 27 years before he died, all on account of a rain at just the right moment. One of the things that help to make life interesting.

I knew another man who did business at our office. In 1890, when he was 18 years old, he was living in New York City with his parents, who were very religious. One afternoon at 1 P.M. a stranger spoke to him and wanted to know if he wanted to earn $1.00. The young man said "Yes." The stranger said, "Follow me." He took him to a theatre and remarked, "A boy just quit and I want you to take his place and act a small part in the first act of the show which will start at 2 P.M. This boy acted only a short part in the first act, which part he learned in one hour. After the first act the manager said, "Come back at 8 P.M. tonight," which the boy did. The boy was home at 9 P.M. and he acted his part 12 times that week. At the end of the week he received $6.00, which he gave to his father and mother, telling them how he had earned it. The father and mother were greatly excited that Saturday night and told the boy not to act any more, but the manager had told him to continue with his acting for several weeks ahead. So the father and mother decided to go to that show on Monday night and see the boy act. They saw nothing wrong with it, so the boy traveled with the same show troop for 9 years, as he turned out to be a very good actor. The troop finally moved to Europe, and the manager begged him to continue with the show. The parents objected to this, so the boy later learned the plumbing trade. Years later the actor claimed he had made a big mistake as he greatly enjoyed the theatre, far more than plumbing work.

One of the most interesting tenants our office ever had was a Mrs. John W. or Edith M. Rees. Her husband was an engineer on the railroad. About 1922 they lived in a house they rented from us for more than three years. She had a very large short haired dog that she thought a great deal of and she had taught the dog some tricks. Her husband hated the dog. He told her one day that unless she would get rid of the dog he would leave home. He left her destitute, except for an automobile and a house full of furniture, including a $1,000.00 piano, which she could play, as she played it for me one time. We did not ask her for any rent as we felt sorry for her. She seemed very nice. One day she notified us that she owed us $75.00 back rent and she said she was going to sell her goods at auction in order to pay all her bills and asked us if that would be all right. We did not expect to get the rent as the rent was in her husband's name, and we told her that, but the day after the sale she came in and paid the rent up to date. She stated that her $1,000.00 piano only brought $100.00. Her automobile would not start at the sale on account of a low battery and that only brought $93.00, where if it had started, it might have brought $350.00, so the auctioneer said. Altogether she only got $320.00 net, after the auctioneer was paid. Then she said, "Now I will have to go to work." We said, "What kind of work?" She said there were six different things she could do, or had worked at in the past, among which was six years with Ringlings' Circus as bareback rider. She said she was going to apply for that work. The reason she quit, was because she fell from a horse and hit a stake, breaking four ribs. Then she married Mr. Rees. She left the office after leaving her address, in case we heard of any work for her. We considered her a good honest woman, as she had paid her husband's back rent. We sent our paperhanger to paper several rooms before renting the house. As he started to go for dinner, the Rees dog was on the porch and would not let him out. So he went without his dinner, rather than take a chance, but the dog went away at four o'clock.

Less than three months later Mrs. Rees was found dead in a $5.00 per month attic room, which she rented from an Italian family one half block west from where she moved out. The dog was with her when she died. The police broke the door down, which was locked, in order to find out what was wrong, as the dog had whimpered for more than two days. There were not more than a few articles of furniture she had kept for this room. On the wall was an extra large framed picture of herself, standing on the backs of two horses, with two other horses in front and one ahead. She held the lines in one hand and a long whip in the other, driving five horses. Then I remembered seeing that act in Ringling's Circus years before and she was the girl who drove that five horse team, twice around the arena, just before the Chariot Races. She died in a lonely room, alone with her friend, the dog, with only an oil lamp for light. But she had in the past performed for, and thrilled millions of people before the bright lights of Ringling Brothers' Circus. In the dresser drawer the police found a note stating that in case of her death, she wanted to be cremated, together with her dog; the ashes of both she wanted scattered on Lake Michigan two miles out from the Chicago River, as Chicago was her former home. This was all seen to by the undertaker because the dresser drawer contained enough money for all expenses. That was the ending of the life of a wonderful circus woman. I afterwards tried to buy that picture from the woman who held the small amount of furni-

Charles Fieldhouse's first boat.

ture, but she said, "After Mrs. Rees' death the husband returned and took the picture with him to Chicago."

During the first World War, George Sheaf came in the office early one morning. His son, Harold Sheaf was overseas. George Sheaf was a man who had both legs off close to his body, as he was run over by a locomotive during his railroad career. This accident happened late at night. The doctor at that time performed the operation by lantern light on a desk in a little railroad office, as Elkhart at that time had no hospital. George many years rode in a wheel chair propelled by two cranks, operated by his two arms, as they were extra strong on account of such exercise. He had two short crutches, so he could climb out of the chair and go in and out of buildings, and climb stairs, so he could go anywhere he wished to. He was a familiar sight on the streets of Elkhart for many years and made his own living during his lifetime by doing work that he could do. This particular morning George Sheaf said to John Fieldhouse, "John, I am in very deep trouble. My wife's mother has been paralyzed for three years and my wife has taken care of her, and this morning at five o'clock my wife had a stroke. What am I to do? My boy Harold is overseas in France as a soldier, and I need him so badly, far more than the government needs him." John said to me, "Charlie, put letter paper in the typewriter."

He then wrote a letter to the War Department at Washington, D.C., and fully explained George Sheaf's unusual situation in Elkhart, and asked that his boy be returned to Elkhart from France. In less than thirty days the boy was back in Elkhart. He was the only soldier on the transport returning from France, while the boats going east were filled with soldiers. This greatly helped George Sheaf out in time of trouble.

George Sheaf's son is still reading water meters for the Elkhart Water Company, which job he has held for 35 years. He has walked more miles than any man I know and knows just where every water meter is in the City of Elkhart. The local Gas Company in Elkhart seems to have a different gas meter reader every month. As we heat our office with gas, each month someone asks us where our gas meter is. I recently told the local manager of the Gas Company of this situation and asked him why they did not have a steady man for reading meters like the Water Company had. His reply was, "Send me that kind of man and I will hire him." I could not think of anyone I could recommend, as that type is unusual.

One day 20 years ago while I was waiting on a young man about 22 years old, who was making a monthly payment on his father's contract, the phone rang. A man from the American Coating Mills asked me if I knew a good young man who would be glad to learn a trade and would be willing to stick with it after he learned it. I turned to young Johnson, and asked him if he had a job. He said "No." I asked him if he would like to learn a trade and stick to it. He said "Yes." I sent him to the man and Johnson has been working there steady ever since. So often a little circumstance like that changes a man's whole life.

One time John wanted to buy a property at auction, sealed bids. He wrote down his price at $5001.00. When all the bids were opened it was discovered there were two other bids at $5,000.00. John got the property on account of the extra dollar. At a similar auction a few months later, there were two bids that had the price $5.00 and $10.00 extra above the even figure. They were trying to buy the property as John did, and the extra $10.00 got it.

When I was nine years old, my father and I stopped at Mehl Benham's livery stable. Mehl was leaning back against the wall in a chair and his cigar ashes had fallen all over the front of his vest. My father said to me, "Look at that, Charlie. If you never smoke or drink until you are twenty one years old, I will give you $500.00." Mehl Benham said, "If Charlies does not smoke or drink until he is twenty one, he never will, because by then he will have brains enough and will know enough to leave them alone." When I came down to breakfast the morning I was twenty one, my plate was upside down. Under it were twenty five $20.00 gold pieces. I have never tasted beer or whiskey and never had a cigarette or cigar in my mouth, largely on account of Mehl Benham's remark.

Also when I was nine years old, one of John's carpenters said to him one day, "Let me make Charlie a boat for the pond." We had boat for breakfast, dinner and supper for two weeks, when John told the carpenter to make it, with boathouse for a pond 250 feet by 150 feet, six blocks from our home. In the deepest place the water was only three feet deep. There were six islands in the pond, with large sycamore trees on each, as the dirt was not dug out where the trees were. In winter it was a popular skating place. I had more boy friends then than I have now.

Three years later, one day, when I was in the boat on the pond, a teamster dumped a load of ashes on the edge of the pond. A month later there were 4 or 5 loads, three years later the pond was completely filled with dirt and ashes, as it was a centrally located spot. John regretted this after the pond was filled, as the pond used to be a beautiful one.

At the ages of nine and ten I was water boy during the summer for the shovelers and teamsters, for which I received 25 cents a day. When I was eleven, twelve and thirteen I worked at carpenter work, nailing on patent lath boards for plaster for three years. By the time I was twenty one I owned a small modern 6 room house on the bank of the St. Joseph River, and had it all paid for from my earnings before I was twenty one. While I was helping on carpenter work on this house, one of the carpenters remarked, "This is the pleasantest place I ever worked." That made me do some thinking. That night I asked a price from John, and he gave me a cost price, so I took it and have had it steadily rented ever since. My work as a carpenter built up my strength so that I was the strongest boy on the school ground for my age. My first year I was paid fifty cents a day, my second year seventy five cents and the third year one dollar a day.

About the year 1895, The Elkhart National Bank could not get their big safe open. They sent to Chicago for a safe expert, who finally ordered the big safe moved out of the building to the yard back of the Fieldhouse office. Much time was spent drilling the iron work, which ruined the safe. Finally after the doors were opened, it was discovered that if the electric current had been left turned on for 15 minutes more, the safe could have been opened, for during the night the electric current was off, unknown to the cashier.

One time John sold Hub Beardsley $5,000.00 of American Coating mill 8% bonds, as an investment. One day, six months later Hub came in and wanted the 5 bonds, which we did not have. He said we did, as we had never made the delivery to him. We spent one full day looking for those bonds and notified Hub we could not find them. Then he came in and wanted his money back. The argument ended in a verbal fight and Hub went out mad. He did not come in again for nearly two years, where he usually called three or four times a year. When he did finally appear, I said to him, "Mr. Beardsley, did you ever find those 5 American Coating Mill bonds?" He said, "Yes." Then I said to him, "Where did you find them?" He said, "When I bought the bonds, I evidently borrowed the money to pay for them from the First National Bank. A year later, when the bank notified me the interest was due, I paid the note and when they gave me the note, they gave me the bonds." These mixups occur often, when one is in business.

One time John sold a $4,000.00 property for a widow, who was a great gossip. She said, "Give me your note drawing 4% interest," which John did. At the end of the year she came in for her interest, which she used to live on. The note ran for fully 15 years. One day she came in and wanted the interest for one year, $144.00, plus the principal, which we figured at $3,600.00, so we gave her a check for $3,744.00. She said, "The total should be $4,160.00." We showed her an endorsement of $400.00 paid her on the principal four years back. She denied she ever got it. I spent two whole days looking for a cancelled check, or for a receipt, but could find neither. We knew if we paid her, that she would broadcast that we tried to beat her out of $400.00, so we decided to stand pat on this situation. She came in altogether four times. The last time she brought in her lawyer and claimed they were going to sue for the total amount. As John was trying to reason with her, she made this remark, "Mr. Fieldhouse, what could I have used $400.00 for, as I don't spend any money above my living?" When she made that remark, I thought, what could she have spent that money for? I happened to think of her house and like a stroke of lightning I had the answer. "Mrs. Chatterdon, about four years ago you built a new front porch on your house, didn't you?" She said, "Yes, that explains everything, as Mr. Kurtz built the porch and when finished he wanted cash, instead of a check, and Charlie brought it down and endorsed the payment on the note."

In the back room of this office is an oil painting, which has hung there for forty years. Before that it had hung in a livery stable for twenty years. At the time it was painted there were no automobiles and the woman who painted it lived in Vistula, 15 miles northeast of Elkhart. The picture is three and a half feet high and six feet long and shows three saddle horses. When the livery stable was discontinued John bought the picture, as the former liveryman had no place to hang it in his home and John had always admired it. The woman who painted it, used to paint spots on horses that her husband stole. Then they would turn the stolen horses out in their pasture field and the original owner would not recognize his stolen horse. It took three years before this was discovered, after which the husband served time for stealing horses.

Will Mann, a local coal dealer in Elkhart, about the same time, had coal stolen from his coal yard quite often. He hired James Longsdorf, a perfectly honest man, to watch his yard at night, but James never found the guilty party. Coal was stolen nearly every night. Someone told Mann to get a thief to watch the yard at night, if he wanted to catch the thief. The same day Will saw a man he knew would steal and asked him to watch his yard. This fellow caught the thief the very first night, for he knew what a thief would do to steal coal and just how he would do it.

About 1925 the Elkhart Water Company lost $458.63 in currency from their vault one night and it was all written up in the local paper about the robbery, but it did not state how the thief got into the safe. So the following day, Elliott Crull, the manager of the water company came in our office and we asked him the question.

He stated the office girl had the combination of the safe written down on a paper on her desk and someone working for the water company evidently found it. John said to Crull, the chances are that the thief has hidden the money in the water company basement, until the excitement is over, then in thirty days he will take it home. That afternoon Crull spent two hours looking through pipe stored in the basement, also looked between every joist in the basement. He left the worst place until last. Finally he laid newspapers on the basement floor, crawled under the work bench, put his arm down a two foot six inch tile that had been set in the cement floor, to carry any small amount of water away in the dirt, so it would slowly drain away. There, at the bottom of the tile, was the $458.63 in cash, even the pennies were there. The next day the front page of the local paper had the story that the money was found, in the item Crull's name was mentioned six times, Fieldhouse's name was not there, as Crull stole all the gravy by taking all credit for the find himself.

John had a 4 story building at 173 E. Marion Street. A complete new heating boiler for steam heat on two floors of the building had just been installed. He sent a man down there with a broom, bushel basket and shovel, and told him to clean the entire building. It took several days to do this and when he had finished there was much waste paper and trash to be burned, so the laborer put it in

Charles and Alma Fieldhouse Lake Michigan Boat for five
years "Skipalong."

the firebox and lighted the paper, burned all
the trash he could in the boiler, without putting water in it, after which the entire boiler
had to be sold to a junk dealer. Another new
boiler had to be installed and paid for. A
written note on the boiler door, might have
saved all this additional expense.

We had a tenant that rented from us for
about twelve years, who got very mad at his
wife and daughter. For a term of about three
years, he never spoke to either of them. He
lived in the basement, tended the fire, worked six days a week, paid the bills, got his own
meals. His wife and daughter both worked,
lived on the main floor and got their own
meals. After three years, they made up again
and afterwards seemed to get along, same
as any other family.

We had one tenant whose wife had walked
in her sleep several times. The husband
wanted a gate hung at the top of the second
floor stairway, so she would not fall down
the stairway, if she walked in her sleep. We
had a gate made and hung by our carpenter.
One night this woman walked in her sleep
after the gate was installed and walked
against the gate which had been put up for
her safety. If the gate had not been there,
she might have been badly hurt.

One time we had a six room house vacant,
that we rented to a man during the winter
who wanted three rooms papered, which
work we did before he moved in. One month

later when he paid the rent, he mentioned that some of the paper in all three rooms had come off. We sent the paperhanger back. He happened to go there on Monday morning and in all three rooms there was live steam, as they were doing laundry work in each room that had been papered. The paperhanger took a count of the people occupying the property. There was a total of twenty three living in that 6 room house, each family occupying two rooms, and all three families were doing laundry work that Monday morning. One family had seven children, another had five children and the third had five, making a total of twenty three persons. They all lived there for a long time, but the rooms were not papered during this tenancy. We never asked the tenants how many children they had, as a large number of children usually behave and are not hard on a house. One child sometimes will be hard on a house, as one child alone often does not behave.

During the depression of 1929 to 1936 we had much trouble getting rents. In 1933, at one time our office had 38 houses vacant and 5 store rooms vacant and besides, we had other properties occupied that were not bringing in rents. In some cases we let these properties be occupied without getting any rent, as many men were out of work and we could not blame them for not paying rent when they had no work. At that time I thought we would always have many vacant

houses, but in 1937 all the houses were filled
again, with all tenants paying and they have
been occupied ever since. In 1948 our office
had 30 callers daily asking for rental houses.
One fourth of them would ask, "What have
you for sale?" We told them we had no vacant houses and we did not try to sell any,
unless we had them vacant, as all such buyers wanted immediate possession. It was too
much trouble to get houses vacant, when
there was no other place for tenants to move
into. At the beginning of the call for rental
houses, we had three tenants who refused to
move, when we asked them to. We offered to
pay their moving expenses plus the first
month's rent. We offered to do this so they
could get a house and vacate our property,
but still they would make no effort to move.
We tried to get one out according to law, but
the Justice of the Peace refused to co-oper-
ate, because when he went out with several
of our men to set the tenant out, the 6 children all began to cry and he did not have the
heart to set them out. Then I told my father, "I know how to get them out," as they
owed 9 months rent. So the next morning
the plumber and I went out. We took all the
plumbing fixtures and hauled them to our
warehouse. In one week I went out to the
house and the tenants were still there. I
told them that if they were not out in three
days, that we would take the windows out.
It happened to be November, and they were

out before the time expired. We immediately rented the house to paying tenants. We used the same plan with the other two tenants and it worked 100% in getting possession. However we had a fourth tenant we did not know we had. During the time when we had many vacant houses we had a caller who wanted to look at a house on Taylor Street. I gave him the key and thought no more about it. Several months later I drove past the house and noticed lace curtains at the windows and thought my father had rented the house. Several months later I noticed there was no name on the rent book for that house, so immediately went to the house to see about it. I could see through the kitchen window four electric plates aglow on the electric stove. I wondered about it, as no one came to the door. We kept extra night lock keys to all our rental houses, so that afternoon I went with two of our carpenters, unlocked the door and here were the people in the house who would not answer the door bell. We all began carrying the furniture out in the street. The man asked, "Which one is the sheriff?" I said, "We don't need any sheriff, as you paid no rent when you moved in." He handed me the key when I asked for it, and as I locked the house, he wanted to go in again. He stayed in the house so long that I went in to see what he was doing. He was taking out a wire he had put around the electric light meter. He had been heating the house by electricity. That system of taking plumbing out we still use today, when we have a tough tenant to deal with, which we sometimes do. They usually don't stay long after the plumbing is removed.

Many times, when people move out and owe rent, which they do not pay when they turn in the keys, they often say, "We will pay the rent we owe later." Ten per cent of them do, ninety per cent of them don't. We always know the ten per cent. For if a man worries about his back rent and comes in often and explains why he cannot pay, that man will afterwards pay if he possibly can. But if he is one that lets us do the walking, that man as a rule will never pay. One man who owed $88.00 when he moved, worried more about it than we did. Three years later he paid it. Six months later, unasked, we wrote him a letter thanking him for the payment. In this letter we wrote that if he ever got hard up again, to let us know, as we would be willing to help him if possible, as we considered him a very honest man. He replied by letter that he would not take $100.00 for that letter, as he would value it in helping his credit as long as he lived. So far he has never asked for a loan, and that letter was written twenty years ago.

About twenty years ago we had a Main Street tenant who got behind on his store rent $300.00 at $100.00 rental per month. We gave him a notice to pay or move. He brought in a friend who signed a personal note with him for $400.00, due in one year. He got behind again, so we had him move. At the end of the year we tried to collect the note but the signer refused to pay it because we had ordered the tenant to move. Three years went by and we still had the note, which we did not feel like suing.

About this time Noah Sassaman, who made a business of collecting, came in the office and J. W. asked him if he could collect that note. He said he would be pleased to try it, if we would give him one fourth of the amount if he collected it, which he thought he could do. J. W. said "O.K., take the note and try it." In just one week he brought in the full amount in currency, which he had collected from the signer. J. W. asked him, "How did you do it?" Noah replied, "I have a friend who has a large moving truck and I pay him $2.00 a trip each evening that I use it. The first night we drove out to the residence of the signer of the note. We drove in his driveway, rang the doorbell and when the signer of the note came to the door, I showed him the note and told him I was a collector, while my friend sat in the truck. He slammed the door in my face, but the next night we made the same trip again. He did not come to the door, so we sat in the truck one hour. We made a total of six trips and the last trip we got the total of $400.00 in currency."

One of the best lessons we ever had in our office was given me by W. F. Stanton. Sometimes we would collect payments, and write a receipt, but, in talking with the customer, we would overlook placing credit on the ledger, which would happen five or six times a year. It always made us feel cheap when we failed to give credit, when a customer brought in his receipt. Stanton usually mailed the check when he paid his women's ready to 'wear store rent, but this time he had a complaint and came personally with his rent check. As he laid the check on the desk, I opened the ledger, marked down the credit on the ledger, then began to write the receipt. As I did so, Stanton said, "That is what I try to get my clerks to do, but they don't always do it." I said, "What is that?" He said, "Write it on the book first, then write the receipt. They sometimes write the receipt and overlook marking it on the book." I said nothing more, but after Stanton went out, I told my father what Stanton said. We both thought it an extra good idea and we both practiced it 100%. Thereafter we never lost any credits on the ledger, for we never touched a receipt book until after we gave credit on the ledger.

One time I wanted to find a man named Eldon Lee, who lived on a large farm of several hundred acres near Wakarusa. I inquired of fully ten persons in Wakarusa as to where I could find him. No one knew, although some said the name sounded familiar. The eleventh person told me, "I don't know Eldon Lee, but Lee Eldon lives just one mile north of Wakarusa." Then I soon found my man.

For a number of years Charles Strong, who was three fourths blind, loafed in the front window of our office two or three times each week. One time he stumbled over a child's cart, left on the sidewalk and got badly hurt, on the way to our office. One day, John said to him, "Look at that tramp across the street, I believe he is drunk." Charles Strong said, "You know, John, I cannot see anyone across the street, on account of my poor eyesight." A half hour later, he said, "Who is that woman walking across the street, John?" John said, "I don't know, but you know, Strong, you could not see the man, but your eyesight is much improved when a woman goes past on the opposite side of the street."

One time, Charles Strong ordered from B. C. Godfrey, a local coal dealer in Elkhart, who was in our office at the time Strong was there, ten tons of coal, which Godfrey later delivered in Strong's basement. Strong would not pay for the coal, as he claimed it was different coal from what he ordered. So Godfrey had his men remove the coal and afterwards put in the kind Strong ordered. But Strong then claimed that according to all the slips, he was 1,000 pounds short. Many arguments afterwards were talked over in this office about that shortage, by Strong and

Godfrey. J. W. told Godfrey to send Strong 1,000 pounds of coal to stop his talking, but Godfrey said, "Then he would talk." Eight years later, they both met in our office and the 1,000 pounds' shortage question came up again. Godfrey finally said, "If I had those slips I could show John Fieldhouse in five minutes that there was no shortage." Strong reached in his pocket and produced the slips. There was no shortage. After Godfrey left, John said to Strong, "Have you been carrying those slips in your pocket for eight years?" Strong said, "You know, John, I have not worn this coat for about 8 years. I just happened to put it on this morning by mistake."

Several years ago I bought a horse fly net, which horses used to wear in warm weather. On my way to the office, I showed it to twelve girls from twelve to fifteen years of age, who were on a front porch. None of these girls could tell what that net was ever used for, which shows that it is a changing world.

When I was a boy, in the horse and buggy days, there were six barns in the block where we lived. One barn held three horses and three grocery delivery wagons. Another boy and I used to help the grocery wagon drivers, by filling stalls with hay, corn and oats, watering and currying the horses, as we enjoyed the work and often took it out in rides. One Halloween night, we put the front wheels in back and the back wheels in front, on all

Charles H. Fieldhouse.

the wagons, as we used to grease the axles once each week. There was 2 inches differences in height. One would hardly notice it unless he saw the side of the wagon a block away. Those three boys drove those wagons three months before they discovered the slant in the wagon box. One of them afterwards told me that he often wondered why he could not turn around on Nadel Avenue any more as he used to do, without backing. No grocery delivery wagons are used these days and there are very few grocery delivery automobiles these days. Yes, it's a changing world.

In all of John Fieldhouse's 55 years of real estate business, he never had a lawsuit. In Charles Fieldhouse's 55 years of real estate business he had three, but he won every one. They were all jury trials. The most interesting one was on account of my buying some ground of the local gas company. When my attorney looked over the abstract, he noticed that the next lot was obtained by Clyde Paxson, just one and a half blocks from the best business location in Elkhart. He got the lot by paying less than $400.00 back taxes, and then, after 2 years, called for his tax deed at the Auditor's Office, which he got. I took it up with the Gas Company, and offered them $1,500.00 more for a quit claim deed on the lot Paxson got away from them, which deed I got.

Six months later I went to see Paxson and told him that for $3,000.00 I would give him a warranty deed for his lot, which would make him a good title, where a tax deed would give him a questionable title. Paxson saw the point and said he would give it, but the same day he found out that I gave $1,500.-00 for the deed I got, so he offered only $2,000.00 after I had made the deal. I just walked out.

Two years later I received notice that Clyde Paxson was beginning a suit to quiet title on the lot. I was at the proceedings with my lawyer and we gave him a fight. On the fourth day of the lawsuit, my attorney told Paxson's attorney that we were going to put a witness on the stand, who would testify that the sale was not made on the Court House steps, according to law, which, if we could prove, would make the tax sale illegal. A recess was asked and my lawyer asked me to go in a private room, where we met Paxson and his lawyer. They wanted our proposition on settlement. I told them that I would take $3,000.00 plus $500.00 attorney's fees. They accepted, so the jury was dismissed, and Paxson got his warranty deed.

Regarding lawsuits, one time, in the horse and buggy days, Ross Bowles, driving a hack, was hit by a train on the Middlebury Street crossing. He sued the Big Four Railway for $10,000.00. For four months Ross walked with a cane and limped each step he took. Each day during the lawsuit he passed our office, on the opposite side of the street, walk-

ing to the interurban, on his way to Goshen.
On the fourth day the lawsuit was settled, the
Railway giving him $2,000.00. The very next
day he walked past on the opposite side of
the street, with no cane and no limp.

About 1907, John had a buyer who paid him
cash for a good lot. The buyer said to him,
"I would like to have a certain contractor
build my house." So John said O.K. This
contractor built a house on the lot, that cost
$7,200.00, which was a lot of money at that
time. The contracting buyer lived in this
house for 15 years. He never paid a dollar on
the principal, but did pay taxes, interest and
insurance each year. One day we averaged
up his account and found the total payments
made did not average what the house would
have rented for during the fifteen years, so
he had the man move and then rented the
property to another party. At the same time,
John had a young man eighteen years old
who bought a hundred dollar lot from him on
a contract, payable at five dollars a month.
The boy lived with his parents and worked
at the Elkhart Rubber Plant. Instead of five
dollars he paid twenty five dollars monthly,
and got four lots altogether. The boy then
bought a 3 room house from the railroad company and moved it on one lot. John loaned
him money to buy materials, and the young
man did the work evenings. When it was finished, he got married and moved in.

Two years later he wanted a loan to build

a better house. John loaned him the money and just about the time he was ready to move in, the boy sold the house and lot on contract at a profit of $400.00. So he still lived in the three room house. Two years later the man wanted another loan to buy materials for another house. The loan was made and the house was built. But just at the time he was getting ready to move, another man wanted to rent the house, so the young man remained in the three room house. Today this man owns forty-two dwelling houses, which he rents, and has them all paid for. He is retired and lives in Elkhart eight months and in Florida four months of each year. The man who bought the lot in 1907 and had a $7,200.00 house built is still renting. The one started at the top of the ladder and went down while the other man started at the bottom of the ladder and went up.

About the year 1920 John Fieldhouse received a four page anonymous letter telling him to leave $10,000.00 in currency under a bridge at Dunlap, five miles south of Elkhart, at midnight on a certain night, otherwise he would not be alive in one week. John paid no attention to the letter, as many words in it were misspelled. John also thought it was written by a certain man who used to work for him, who was sent to Michigan City penitentiary and was just released from there a short time before. So it did not worry John at all.

About a year later W. H. Foster, a well off manufacturer, received the same kind of letter. C. D. Greenleaf happened to tell John that Foster received such a letter and was a little worried about it. So John went over to see Foster's letter and compared it with his. Both letters had been written by the same person, as the same words were misspelled in Foster's letter that were misspelled in John's letter. When John told Foster who the man was, he found that the same man had once worked for Foster, which relieved Foster from further worry. No money was left under the bridge and no one was killed on account of it.

One time I asked Robert E. Proctor, a very successful lawyer in Elkhart, how he could always make a very good speech without any written notes to refer to. He replied that before making a speech he always got well posted on what he was going to talk about. Then he would line up his eight or ten subjects in rotation in his mind. He would never rehearse his speech but would memorize his subjects. In 1938 I was asked to talk for one half hour before an audience on the subject of real estate. I had just 24 hours, so in this time I memorized ten subjects in rotation, and I did not rehearse the speech. Before I talked there were two one half hour speakers ahead of me. Both of these men read their talks from papers they had prepared for the occasion. When my time came, I got up on the platform and talked steadily for thirty minutes without referring to any notes. From the grapevine route I heard that I surprised one woman in the audience. She wondered how I did it without any notes. I could not have done it without the help of Robert E. Proctor.

Where my mother, Mary J. (Hubbard) Fieldhouse, was born in 1851, four miles southwest of the center of Elkhart on a 154 acre farm, they had "No Hunting" signs posted in a 30 acre tract of virgin timber. One November day I was draining the plumbing in the house, built in 1849, which we used as a summer home. About three P.M. I heard a gun go off in the woods, but paid little attention to it. But when I heard two more shots, I immediately started for the woods, searching the entire woods for the hunter. Returning to the house, as I was passing the barn, two more shots were fired close by from the woods. So I went back, but still could find no hunter. As I returned to the barn again I heard two more shots and when I left the woods the last time, it was dark. Two weeks later a neighbor, calling on me at the farm, had a good laugh. He said that a boy at Jamestown, who did not like the idea of those "No Hunting" signs, noticed that I was at the farm that afternoon. He had a 45 caliber revolver with him, so he went in the woods and climbed a tree to a point 40 feet from the ground. Then he began shooting. I went on numerous trips. Each time when he saw that I was at the barn, he shot again. He told Archie Cocanower, the neighbor, that Charles Fieldhouse was a pessimist for all he did was look down as he went through the woods. "If he had looked up, he might have seen me." It perhaps was a good idea that I did not look up, but it taught me something, for I have been looking up ever since.

In 1936 we bought two acres of ground on the Dunes Highway, on the most heavily traveled country road in the world. Lake Michigan is more than 300 miles long, and all travel by road to the west has to come to the foot of Lake Michigan to get to Chicago. A signboard, built in 1936 which is the longest I have ever seen, 110 feet long and 12 feet high, has been there from 1936 to this date, advertising the Hotel Dixie Grande at Bradenton, Florida. For many years the weeds grew in front of this signboard. A number of years ago when I was there, looking the signboard over, a man cutting grass and weeds on the road, stopped his machine and told me that for $15.00 per year, he would keep the grass and weeds mowed in front of the sign. This work improves the looks of the sign greatly. However, it is difficult to know whether this signboard pays or not, as there is no way of checking on it. However we do know that it has brought the hotel some business.

One time we had a house vacated by a tenant who owed four months back rent and when we entered the vacant house, we found all the electric fixtures were missing, only the wires were left to tell the story. We had no idea where the man moved, but I asked every moving van operator, as to whether or not he had moved the tenant. About the sixth person I asked was the man and he told me where the former tenant moved to. I went out to the property, found no one at home, but left a note under the door stating that we would give him forty eight hours to return those fixtures to the house he had vacated. Two days later I went out to the vacant house, found every fixture hanging from the ceiling, even the wires were soldered and wrapped with tape, same as they were before they were taken down.

One time we divided a lot, sold one half to the property owner on each side. But the one party backed out, did not buy his 25 by 132 feet, which made it difficult to sell, as the other party did not care to buy any more than his 25 feet. Several years later a man wanted to rent a vacant piece of ground for storing a trailer on for several months. I showed him this 25 feet and told him there would be no charge for three months, but not to broadcast it. In three days I sold the one half lot to the man who had changed his mind, for he changed his mind again.

Automobiles purchased and used by John

W. Fieldhouse during his lifetime were as
follows: In 1902 John bought a single seated
Mobile Steamer from Terrytown, N. Y.; In
1903 a single cylinder, four passenger Shelby
from Shelby, Ohio. This car made four round
trips to Chicago and back in the two years
that he owned it, a trip of 122 miles one way.
In 1905 he bought a four cylinder, 5 passenger Columbia from Hartford, Conn. John
took the agency for this car and sold eight
Columbia cars in Elkhart during a three
year period. They allowed 20% commission
for selling cars in those days and all a real
estate dealer got in commission for selling
real estate was 3%. At that time John gave
some thought to going out of the real estate
business and going into the automobile business, on account of the extra large commission allowed in selling automobiles. But he
changed his mind largely on account of one
sale. He wired the Columbia Automobile
Company in 1907 that he could sell a $4,000.-
00 car, if they could ship a car immediately.
They wired back they could, although they
were two months behind on their orders.
The auto was here in four days, the varnish
was not yet dry. The engine missed badly
and the owner had nothing but trouble, so
he drove the car back to Hartford, and as the
automobile entered the rear door of the plant,
an employee yelled, "Here comes the old
demonstrator!" The owner of the car heard
the remark and thereby found out that he

Alma C. Fieldhouse.

had bought a second hand automobile. New valves had been placed in the engine, before the automobile was shipped by freight and the new valves did not fit the old seats, which caused the engine to miss. The Columbia Company refused to make a cash settlement on this matter, so John discontinued his agency. However they shortly afterwards went into the hands of a receiver and John bought one of their last cars made in 1908, a four cylinder, seven passenger Columbia, which he used for four years. He drove it to Portland, Maine, and as far west as Denver.

In 1912 he bought an Abbott Detroit, four cylinder, seven passenger with no self starter, but with electric headlights. In 1916 he bought a twelve cylinder Pathfinder, made at Indianapolis. In 1923 he bought an eight cylinder Cadillac. In 1929 he bought an eight cylinder Pierce Arrow, which he drove for 9 years until his death. In addition to the above, in 1913, he bought a Michigan four cylinder automobile for his business car, made at Kalamazoo. In later years he bought a Crow Elkhart, made at Elkhart, plus four Studebakers made at South Bend, also a Dodge car, which he used for business purposes. He often remarked that he wished he had a horse and buggy also, as he had used a team Gyp and Topsy in his business for a period of 18 years up to the year 1913. One day a man came in and wanted to trade a horse and buggy with harness for a lot. In less than one hour the trade was made and John was delighted. He told me to drive the rig over and put the whole outfit in the barn, one block away, which I did. One week later he had to make a trip four miles south, so he told me about one-thirty P.M. to bring the whole outfit over to the office, which I did. John did not come back until five thirty P.M., and came back walking. He said to me, "I felt cheap, driving that outfit down Main Street on the brick paving with those iron tires on the wheels." John had been used to rubber tires on wheels and the iron tires made so much noise that he imagined everyone was looking at him, and they may have been. He sold the whole outfit to a farmer for $100.00. He lost about $200.00 on the deal but he never mentioned thereafter about wanting a horse and buggy. That was his last ride in one, which was about 1916.

In 1920 Samuel T. Gaines from Kentucky, rented the Hotel Bucklen from John Fieldhouse who was Agent for H. E. Bucklen and Gaines made a reputation for serving good meals in the dining room. In one large corner room on the third floor he had twelve men sleeping in one room, as they were strike breakers at Foster Machine Company Plant, which was on a strike. About a hundred employees met at the plant early one morning, so the strike breakers went back to the hotel, and the employees of the Foster Plant followed them. The police were powerless, as some of the men marched up the wide stairway, but on the second floor they met on the stairway landing to the third floor old man Gaines, rather a large man of about seventy years of age. In his hand he had a long butcher knife he had got from the kitchen. He addressed the mob, as follows, "Boys, I have twelve men who have been customers of my hostelry for a number of weeks and I am here to protect them. I have lived for many years in the State of Kentucky. In circumstances such as this, they knife them down there and the first one of you that tries to pass me on this stairway, will get this knife, for I will knife him here, just like they do it in Kentucky." The way Gaines said it, they knew he meant it and they retraced their steps to the lobby and the street. Several weeks later a settlement was made and the plant resumed operations.

A Lake Shore and Michigan Southern engineer came in the office to make a payment one day, many years ago. He was an uneasy man that day. We could tell something bothered him. Before he left he told this story. "Several hours ago I was bringing a freight train from Chicago. At LaPorte I could see a seven year old boy sitting on the ties of our track about half way between the rails, several hundred feet ahead. I was going about 15 miles an hour and could do nothing but blow the whistle. The boy had his foot caught in the end of an upright iron pipe, below the ties. He could not free himself, but struggled to do so in his sitting position. The cow catcher struck him near the center of his body, and instantly killed him. If the boy had lain back on the ties with his head down, the train would have passed over him and he would have lived, without a scratch.

Around the year 1950, our office had about 30 people every day, asking if we had a house for rent, but we only averaged one vacant about every three months, so a good many people were disappointed. We had some homes that were occupied by three families, but we did not object, as it was helping out in a way. Many people were making conditions bad by overcharging on rent, as they knew houses were scarce. The worst one I knew of was three rooms over a grocery store, with an outside stairway. The grocery-man charged this family with three children $100.00 per month and would not allow the children to play in the yard below. This mother had to work also as a waitress at a local hotel, in order to help pay the rent. The husband worked days and his wife worked nights and in this way the father and mother did not have to hire any help to look after the children. One afternoon the mother with three children got home with some groceries from the A & P. After they got upstairs, up came the groceryman and he informed her that thereafter, as long as she was renting from him, she was supposed to buy her groceries down stairs. I had a six room dwelling next to this store, all modern with garage, which rented for $17.00 per month. The rooms over the grocery would be high priced at $25.00 per month, but they were renting for $100.00 per month, which to me looked like daylight robbery.

At one time an ash hauler, a single man twenty seven years old, called at our office and told me that he had found a man's suit done up in a newspaper on top of an ash pile he was hauling away for the owner of the rental property. The next morning he put on the suit and decided to wear it, but in wearing it, he noticed something in the lining of the coat. When he returned to his room that night, he took a knife and cut the lining and found $400.00 in currency. He took the money to the man he was working for and told him that the money evidently belonged to his tenant whose husband had died several weeks before. The ash hauler told him to deliver her the $400.00 and tell her that the ash hauler had found it. But the property owner immediately divided the money into two separate piles of $200.00 each, gave half to the ash hauler and he kept half, telling the ash hauler to "keep his trap shut."

The ash hauler quit work, spent the money foolishly and then came to me with his story, as he wanted to get it off his mind. I said to him, "If you had returned all the money to the widow and had told me about it, your name would have been in big type on the front page at the top of the Elkhart Truth as follows, "Ash hauler finds $400.00 in an old suit left on an ash pile and returned the money." You would have been sized up as a perfectly honest man, and you might have been offered a far better job than hauling ashes, as honest men are what some people are looking for."

One time Vitas Stanley, our electrician, went to a house to put in a buzzer button under the dining room table. Under the rug he found $400.00 in currency. He laid it aside, but when he got through he placed the money under the rug on the opposite side of the room as a joke. Three weeks later the woman of the house left orders for Mr. Stanley to come and see her immediately, which he did. She scolded him for stealing that money, and told him she was going to have him arrested, unless he brought it back. Mr. Stanley stepped into the dining room, turned the opposite side of the rug back and there was the $400.00. The woman had no more to say when she found Vitas Stanley was honest. Mr. Stanley afterwards found $520.00 in currency hidden in a basement where he was working and handed the amount to the woman occupying the house. She seemed surprised and made no remark, but took the money.

One time, a number of years ago, a local Realty Company was trying to get road number 33 past their addition, which was then undeveloped, and by making numerous trips to Indianapolis, they were succeeding, according to the local papers. My father was greatly opposed to this change, as road 33 would pass many cross streets, whereas on the other route there was only one cross street, in a distance of two miles. My father got a number of large heavy sheets of drawing paper, and I went to work making a perfect drawing of both roadways, showing all streets on both routes, which took me two days to complete, four maps in all, two duplicates. Then we wrote two separate letters to Indianapolis, one to the Governor's office and one to the Surveyor's office, and we told them what we thought. Within ten days the plans were changed and road 33 did not pass the newly laid out addition. It would have, if it had not been for our letters and plans.

We never carried an extra large amount of fire insurance on any of our properties, as we figured, if the fire starts, the fire department usually gets the fire out. Only once in a great while it is a total loss. It is a good idea to inspect one's property frequently, for if one looks for trouble he sometimes finds it. One time in going through a public garage basement, I noticed five bushels of loose excelsior all in one pile. A skating rink occupied the second floor. I spoke to the garage operator about the loose excelsior and he promised to get rid of it before the sun went down that night. But the excelsior remained there for two weeks more and one Sunday afternoon at 2 P.M. it caught on fire when no one was there. A flare was evidently thrown from a broken window 10 feet away, evidently by the skating rink tenant, who had $6,000.00 of fire insurance on his few belongings, not worth more than $600.00. Someone saw the smoke coming from the Main Street basement window and turned in a fire alarm. The total loss was only $800.00, but if the fire had not been promptly reported, the skating rink tenant might have gotten $6,000.00. Just last week I went through the Bucklen Theatre Building and found a three foot high waste paper basket, overflowing with paper, in the hallway on the second floor. I immediately took it down to another tenant's furnace and burned it all. I discovered in the center of the basket a large oil soaked rag, which might have caused a fire from combustion. There are also such things as fire bugs. They are scarce, but we do have them, both men and boys. Back of the office there once was a stairway attached to another building and under this stairway was much rubbish, waste paper and pasteboard boxes and excelsior. One evening just after dark, I was seated on our front porch at the residence, when I noticed a bonfire in that alley. When I got there the entire stairway was ablaze. What set it on fire? Some fire bug, in my opinion, as all it needed was a lighted match.

One time my furnace man, Charles Brugg-

ner, told me that my furnace expense on
bungalows would be greatly reduced, if I
filled the attic of each bungalow with about
four inches of rock wool, so I ordered this
work done. At that time the average cost
was $125.00 per house and it immediately
paid dividends. For doing this work I did not
raise one rent and the total cost was more
than $6,000.00. Bruggner's idea was, that
when the house got warm, they would shut
off the draft, and would not overheat the
castings, where if the house was cold the tenant would keep the draft on. One cold winter
day in February, I noticed two of these bungalows side by side, had 5 inches of snow on
their roofs. One block away was a bungalow
that had no snow on the roof, and I wondered
why. I discovered that this bungalow had no
rock wool in the attic, as it had been overlooked. On February 15th rock wool was put
in and in the spring the tenant said they had
one and a half tons of coal left which they
would not have had if rock wool had not been
added.

I have found that storm windows are also
a great coal saver and if left on the year
around, they make a house warmer in winter
and cooler in summer.

Sam Dudley is a locksmith who lives in a
basement room of Hotel Bucklen and has his
key shop there also. In getting some keys
made there one day, I said to Sam, "My, but
your plate glass windows are dirty and they

All ready for Michigan City, in the good old summertime.

have been that way for several years. Why
don't you wash them?" Sam said, "I will tell
you why. When I first moved here twelve
years ago, my rent was $12.50 per month.
After I cleaned the place up, my rent was
$20.00, three years later they raised it again
to $25.00, three years later they raised it to
$30.00 and two years ago they raised it to
$35.00. Now if I painted the room and wash-
ed the windows, they would raise the rent to
$50.00, so I am letting everything go, so my
rent won't be raised again." Sam had the
right idea, I guess.

Our office had six safes for many years,
most of them containing abstracts. We never had a safe opened by bandits during 73
years, as they would not know which safe to
open. One winter night, however, when I
was alone in the office, working on the books
about 8 P.M., I had the front door locked, as
it was six below zero and I knew I would
have no callers that cold evening. I heard
a man whistling as he crossed the street towards the office. He had no coat or vest on,
just a white shirt. He opened the outside
door, then tried the inside door and found it
locked. He immediately turned and ran
across the street to an alley. There was no
question but what he would have held me up
if the door had been unlocked, so I have always kept the door locked on dull nights.

Mrs. Lamb, who operates the abstract office close to our office, told me one time,

"Charles Fieldhouse, some night you are going to be held up when you are alone in the office." I said nothing, but one night when she passed by, I motioned her to come in and she found the door locked. On account of this man trying the door, I afterwards installed an air tank in the basement, with 100 pounds of air furnished by an electric air pump. In the office I installed a steam boat whistle, connected with the pipe from the tank. I had a special pulley made, connected with a large brass valve. From the pulley was a wire cable which held a 125 pound weight. By pushing the rod down three inches it would release the weight which would drop and jerk valve open, when an extra loud whistle would blow. I never feared bandits after this system was installed. It is still in operation waiting for them.

John Hite recently had such a system at his sporting goods store north of Elkhart. Two 17 year old boys broke in the back window at one o'clock one night, picked out a new revolver, plus bullets and looked around the other merchandise to see what they wanted. While they were looking around they stepped on a certain spot on the floor where an electric alarm was located and set off a large electric bell. The boys were so scared when this bell rang and twelve electric flood lamps lighted the entire room, they went right through the large plate glass window in front of the store. They were badly cut by broken glass and were captured on account of the trail of blood they left. John had a special electric bell in the dwelling house to the north and that woman called the police.

About 1945 I had a cement boat house built by a local contractor, Ira Mast, all of poured concrete and it was made so a boat could float within. The first winter the renter reported that the launch had a coat of ice all over it half an inch thick, as there was no ventilation. The next spring I had Andy Peterson, a stone mason, cut two six inch round holes through the ten inch walls on two sides of the boathouse to ventilate it, which did the trick. His bill was for eight days work, plus a $13.00 blacksmith bill for sharpening his tools. When I asked him why the blacksmith bill was so high and his time was so many hours, his reply was, "Whoever built that boathouse used an extra good mixture of cement, as it was the hardest cement that I have ever encountered." Ira Mast built this boathouse on a contract. He could easily have cheapened the mixture and thereby made more money. On account of this discovery I have since given him a great deal of work, as I have much confidence in him, for he takes pride in his work. I have paid him more than $100,000.00 for work he has done for me since, largely on account of his honesty on the boathouse job.

About the year 1949, my wife and I visited Friendship Gardens at Michigan City, a tract of about 100 acres with beautiful gardens representing many countries. There is an island in the park used as a stage, with a pond of water around it. Along a little narrow stream were about fifty willow trees fully fifty feet high. There were also many flowers in bloom, in fact it is a beautiful park. As we came out of the place about an hour later, the ticket man asked where we were from. I told him "Elkhart." He asked what kind of business I was in and I told him "real estate" and that my name was Fieldhouse. Then he said "Mr. Fieldhouse, I was in your office years ago when this place first started and I asked your father if I could take some sprouts from a willow tree that he had in a yard back of one of his houses. He told me to take all that I wanted, without any charge, so I did. I stuck the sprouts in the ground near the water in this park and here are the trees to-day, all from just one day's work. The reason they grew fast, the top of the ground was close to water level, and not one died.

In 1949 I bought a small number of acres in the heart of Michigan City on a river called Trail Creek, a quarter mile from Lake Michigan. Here we had a boathouse built. At the same time I ordered a 33 foot steel cabin cruiser, at Saginaw, Michigan, with two 100 H.P. engines. We did not get spring delivery, as the boat we were to get was delivered in the spring to another party. We did not get out boat until after the middle of June the next year. About June 28th, 1950, we left in the boat for Michigan City, a trip of about 600 miles, and were 7 days making the trip. The entire trip was in rough water, with waves as high as four and five feet, on account of windy weather. Our first night's stop was at East Tawas, next night at Alpena, then Sheboygan, then Charlevoix, Frankfort, Pentwater, Saugatuck and Michigan City, our home port.

Every morning, including the first morning, we had much trouble in starting the two engines. One we called the hoodoo, as we had to take the twelve sparkplugs out and prime the cylinders, sometimes several times. We noticed that the electric starters turned the engines very slowly and we also noticed the fittings on one engine were different than the other, but each morning we got them both started. After they were warmed up they started easily but when cold we always had trouble starting them.

Many times at Michigan City, we started out with only one engine, rather than bother starting the hoodoo engine. In three years' time we were out on Lake Michigan several times, with both engines dead. The last time we were pulled in by the Coast Guard. We decided to get new engines from a firm at Coldwater, Michigan. We got two new four cylinder 50 H.P. engines, which we liked much better, as they burned far less gas and made the boat run quietly at a speed of about

14 miles an hour, instead of 20. In trading in the old engines. I told the dealer that one was a hoodoo. He allowed me $500.00 for both of them. They cost me $1,800.00. Two weeks later he wrote me that the hoodoo engine was a very old engine, and that both engines were worn out. The hoodoo he was going to sell for junk. He said someone had inflicted me with second hand engines. Both motors had been freshly painted to look like new. So Alma and I had much boating trouble on account of one man.

After having the boat five years, we were rather tired of making so many trips of fifty miles each way between Elkhart and Michigan City, so, at a cost of $155.00 we placed one advertisement in the Chicago Tribune, three inches by four inches, using one half the space for a picture of the boat and the other half for a description of it. We received a total of seven letters and out of the seven we had three cash buyers. I wrote them all that we would be at the boathouse from 1 to 6 P.M. on the following Sunday afternoon. Five carloads came to look the boat over and in two hours we had it sold for $4,900.00, the price quoted in the paper. We delivered the boat, with the man and his wife who purchased it and crossed Lake Michigan to the Calumet River in Chicago to his docking space which was eight miles up the river. We went under 14 bridges on our trip up the Calumet River. On the eight mile trip up the river, we found industry all the way, which made it a very interesting trip.

In making many trips from Elkhart to Michigan City and back, we crossed the Michiana crossing of the Michigan Central Railroad, which was 5 miles east of Michigan City, in order to drive five miles along the lake past many summer cottages along the south shore of Lake Michigan. This crossing was the most dangerous railroad crossing that we ever encountered, as it was over a steep hill between the Dunes Highway and the railroad, with a dangerous curve in the railroad to the east. The railroad flashers were too high on account of the hill and could not be seen by a driver coming from the east over the Dunes Highway. We were always careful each time we crossed here. One Sunday we saw an automobile almost get hit by a speeding passenger train on this crossing. The next day I wrote the Michigan Central Railroad Company at Chicago and told them there were four things wrong with their Michiana Crossing. I received a nice letter from one of the officials. I afterwards sent him eight pictures which I took with my camera. For each picture, I waited for a car to go over the crossing, in order to show the slant of the hill. As I was taking these eight pictures a strange woman came up to me and said, "Why are you taking so many pictures of this crossing?" I told her, because I thought it was a dangerous one. Then she said, "Did you say dangerous crossing?" I said "Yes." She said, "Do you know how many people have been killed on this crossing in ten years, since I have lived here?" I said, "Ten?" She said, "Nearly a hundred, as every year this crossing takes its toll. They have talked about an underpass, but the County has to pay 65% of the cost, and the County is bonded to the limit of the law, so they keep on killing people, sometimes six in one carload."

I wrote this to the railroad official when I sent him the pictures. I received a total of five letters from him in regard to the crossing. I don't know if my letters helped or not, but two and a half years later the crossing was fenced up and abandoned, and a new modern crossing was made two thousand feet west, nearer Michigan City, with electric bell, electric flashers and automatic gates. If anyone gets killed on the new crossing, it will not be the railroad company's fault. One resident told me since, that six lives were lost on the Michiana Crossing in the two and a half years before they changed it, or from the time I wrote them the first letters to the time the crossing was changed. My father often wrote letters when he noticed something was wrong and I have followed in his footsteps. A number of times our letters have paid dividends.

John one time sold a property to a man on contract who was a great man to complain.

In a way, we used to hate to see him come in, as he never had a good word for anybody, but always found fault, everything was wrong. One day years later, after he had paid out in full, he fell on an icy sidewalk and broke his leg. Mrs. Reynolds who was a reader in the Christian Science Church saw him fall and each day for five months she called at his home and talked and read Christian Science to him. After five months he was a different man. He never found fault about anything, but always talked as if everything was all right. Christian Science changed that man's thoughts completely, as always thereafter he had a good word for everybody.

John one time sold a residence to a man for $4,000.00. The man paid $500.00 down and the balance was payable monthly, which could be for a period of about ten years. The man however paid extra large payments every month. In a little over three years he had the property all paid for. John said to him, "You paid out in a hurry." The man replied, "Well, you see, Mr. Fieldhouse, I hold two jobs. I work for the Indiana & Michigan Electric Company five and a half days a week, reading electric light meters. Then I work for the New York Central Railway Company, six days a week, so I am making good money." This man held both of those jobs for a period of about four years. Then he had a breakdown, and his health

A one cylinder. No room for hitchhikers.

failed. The doctor told him to sit still day after day, week after week and month after month. He partly recovered and is still living today, doing light work. The trouble was, when he was working both jobs, his sleep each day was less than five hours out of twenty four, excepting Sundays. He nearly lost his life on account of being too ambitious. He did not give his heart enough rest.

In 1907 John had a man working for him who claimed he was badly hurt helping construct a new sewer. John would not settle with him, as he had no liability insurance. About the sixth time he was in the office on crutches, he told John that he was going to hire a lawyer, unless he settled that day. John then told him he would make settlement as soon as he could walk to the office without crutches, but not before. On the following day John found this man working on another sewer job, and the crutches were not with him. The man never came in the office again.

William Renn was a railroad man who retired as locomotive engineer at the age of sixty five. A writeup in the paper stated he had railroaded for forty seven years and had never been in one accident. John Longacher met him on the street the next day and congratulated him on his good luck. Renn then said that the N.Y.C. Ry. President did not call it good luck, he called it good judgment.

About twenty five years ago, father, mother and I picked up a shell-shocked hitchhiker.

We hauled him twenty five miles. He was the last hitchhiker we ever picked up, for we learned a lesson that day.

In 1910 I was working with a very successful machine shop manufacturer, William H. Foster, who said he could straighten the steel frame of father's automobile, with my help. We were both working on the frame, when the jacks both slipped out of place, letting the front part of the car drop two feet to the floor. After the work was finished and we were picking up the tools on the floor, I said to Foster, "That was the first time I ever witnessed such an accident that I did not hear some swear words, when the car fell, but I did not even hear a grunt." To which Foster replied, "Swearing would have only made matters worse." How true that remark was.

My father bought a good lounge once at Marsh₋'l Field's Store in Chicago. He ordered it snipped to Elkhart, then inquired what floor the men's suit department was on. Twenty minutes later the clerk that sold him the lounge came to the suit department and told John to make another check for $120.00 less, as the lounge was marked down and he did not know it. That is what I call an unusually good store, no wonder they have been in business so many years.

One time we had a number of houses vacant. One of our best tenants said he was going to buy a nice residence on the St. Joseph River at Bristol. We were very sorry to hear it. One hour later John told me to put a letter in the typewriter addressed to Dr. Rex Douglas, the man who was going to move to Bristol, which is ten miles from Elkhart. John wrote him it would take twenty minutes to go from Elkhart to Bristol. In ten years, counting only three hundred days in the year and counting twenty minutes each way, you will have traveled sixty thousand miles and you will have spent two thousand hours. In twenty years, one hundred twenty thousand miles and you will have spent four thousand hours. In thirty years one hundred eighty thousand miles and you will have spent six thousand hours. After the doctor got the letter, he changed his mind about buying the property at Bristol and he remained our tenant for a number of years.

One time John sold an inside piece of property to a man who was going to build an industrial building on it. That was when the zoning law had just started. The buyer found out he had to get 70% of the property owners to sign his petition within a three hundred foot radius of his property. After working two weeks in trying to get them he lacked thirty one feet of having enough signers. He wanted John to take the property back. John said, "Did Mrs. Niman sign?" He said "No, because she is a special friend of a neighbor and she told her not to sign." John said, "Mr Smith, go to the bank and get a $200.00 check cashed in five dollar bills. Then ring Mrs. Niman's door bell and ask to see her dining room table. Then place those five dollar bills all over her table in a single layer. Then say to her, "If you sign here you can keep the money on the table." She quickly signed, and the building was built.

One time in talking to a young man who was talking about buying a home, I asked him if he wanted a garage built on the lot. He replied that he never would want a garage, as his first wife was killed in an automobile on the New Carlisle railroad crossing. On that account he made a vow he would never ride in an automobile again, as he too was in that accident with a broken leg and arm. He did not see the train until it was ten feet from them.

One day we received a letter from New York City asking if the Woolworth store building could be bought. I went to the owner and found out the building could not be bought. So I wrote New York that the Woolworth building could not be bought, but the Nellie Hill building which was the same size and only one block north could be bought and gave them the price. They wrote me to count the women shoppers for 15 minutes passing both buildings at the same time. This was done from two thirty P.M. to two forty five P.M. The Woolworth building had two hundred forty four, the Hill building had seventy six. That man knew real estate.

One time O. P. Bassett who sold out his Daily Review newspaper to the Elkhart Truth, with my father as agent, traveled around for four months trying to buy another newspaper in another city of about ten thousand population, so he would not have a competitive newspaper. He asked me one day what city of ten thousand population I would choose. One city was in Indiana, one in Ohio, one in Illinois and one in Wisconsin. I told Mr. Bassett, "I would not choose any of them. You know how to play the piano; you are a musician and a business man. W. J. Gronert died recently so why don't you buy Mr. Gronert's "Martin Band Instrument" factory stock, with the understanding that you manage that factory, as it is now without a helmsman." Bassett said nothing but he immediately left the office and four days later I read in the Elkhart Truth that O. P. Bassett had bought the W. J. Gronert stock and was to be the manager of that plant. Bassett lived nine years and at his death his estate was worth many times what it would have been if he had bought a newspaper in a small city.

Mr. Crate Williams, a local house mover in Elkhart fifty years ago moved a very large nine room brick house seventy five feet, and turned it a quarter way around for my father without damaging the walls in any way.

He had long timbers in those days for such work.

One time the three story and basement building occupied by Sykes Department Store caught on fire. This was just a block from where we lived. As I got in the store, the fire was going up the elevator shaft at a rapid rate. I said to the three Sykes brothers, who were the only ones in the store at seven A.M., "Let me take all the silk I can carry over to the store across the street." They all three said, "No." That silk was all destroyed. I could have saved several thousand dollars worth of silk for them, as they did not have enough insurance. They admitted it afterwards, when it was too late.

I almost lost my life in 1907 by starting a four cylinder Columbia automobile engine in a closed barn, as I was regulating the vibrator coils located on the dash. Five minutes more would have killed me from inhaling carbon monoxide gas. The only thing that saved me was that my father came home promptly at twelve o'clock noon for dinner. While I was eating dinner I had a violent headache, which did not leave me until four thirty P.M.

In buying a furnace for a house, we always got a price. Then we would say how much extra for the next size larger. The next size was what we always bought. We also used this same method in buying a stoker for a heating plant.

In painting houses, we always found that chocolate brown paint covered the best and lasted the longest. We bought so much brown paint from a local paint manufacturing company that they used to label some of the paint cans "The Famous Original Bonded Fieldhouse Chocolate Brown."

At one time we leased a store room to Moskin Brothers, a ladies and men's clothing store. Their traveling representative told us they had one hundred and thirty nine stores in their chain at that time and that he had our lease with him all the time, as it was the shortest lease they had, but still it told everything and there were only eleven lines. One store building owner brought out a ten page lease. He showed him our lease, after which he shortened his lease to only four pages. All of our leases are short, also our deeds, contracts and letters.

We had a tenant who moved out of a house owing sixty four dollars rent. He afterwards paid it by paying from twenty-five cents to two dollars per week until it was all paid.

We bought a house once which we rented to a tenant who got typhoid fever. Later another member of the family had it, then the third member of the family had it. They all recovered and afterwards moved out. When we rented the house again, the new tenant found the kitchen sink was stopped up. Our plumber discovered the water ran into a double barrel, one on top of the other, which was underground, just outside the wall from the sink. The screen to the well pump was just three feet below the bottom of the drainage barrel. This was the source of the typhoid fever.

In my father's Fourth Addition there were two flowing wells he had driven. One operated for thirty years, the other flowed for forty years. The water from these wells was very good and many people came to these wells for drinking water. At another place in the addition a spring developed at the base of a twenty foot hill. Many people went there for drinking water and one claimed it was curing his rheumatism. One day the manager of the Elkhart Water Company visited the spring. He knew there was a city water main underground at that point. He had a man dig there the next day and found a leak in the water pipe which caused what people thought was a spring.

In 1893 during the Chicago Worlds' Fair, my father sent two carpenters there early in the spring and had them build a 6 room cottage. He put ten cots in it. We were there two weeks during the Fair. The rest of the time the keys were turned over to all the relatives on both sides, each of whom occupied the cottage for one week. The cottage is still there on 61st Street and when I pass it now and then, I can distinguish the old Fieldhouse pattern.

Three years ago one of my renters thought he would go to Wisconsin and shoot a deer, as one of his neighbors had done the year before. So he bought a red shirt and cap for fifteen dollars plus eight dollars for a license. He drove alone six hundred and fifty miles and found a suitable woods where he sat for two hours on a three foot log, waiting for a deer to come along. A shot rang out, the bullet missed him by only three feet and struck a tree ten feet away. He hollered and yelled, so another shot would not be fired. He walked to his car and headed for Elkhart, Indiana. That man will never go hunting again.

We had a house once which stood vacant for six months. Many people looked at it, but it did not rent. One day I took a party to look at it. I noticed all the windows were very dirty. The same week I had all the windows washed inside and out. The house was immediately rented. Washing windows often pays dividends. When you want to sell a house, new window shades with good curtain rods greatly help also.

Some of our houses in the past have developed termites. We have always gotten rid of them by using creosote and kerosene sprayed on in the basement where they usually are found.

One time we had a contractor trying to pull some long piling which he finally gave up, as he said it could not be done. Another man

The Mill will never grind again, with the water that has passed. High Dive Swimming Pool, Elkhart, Indiana. "The Place of Happiness."

told me he could do it, which he did. The first man tried to pull them straight up with a high derrick, but suction held them. The second man pulled them out sideways, where suction did not hold. It is very easy when one knows how.

One time my father attended a National Realestate Convention at New Orleans. A special friend of his told him he was going to make a five minute speech on his home city and he thought he would get the $1,000.00 prize. He got it. My father said to him, "Your speech was wonderful. How did you know you were going to get the prize?" "Be cause I spent six months writing that speech and I spent six months learning it and re- hearsing it once each night."

One day Willard Chester, a well known lawyer, and Charles Drake, a well known merchant, came in father's office and said to him, "Mr. Fieldhouse, we would like to bor- row $150,000.00." To which my father re- plied, "I never make small loans." They walk- ed out two inches shorter than when they came in.

My mother was well acquainted with a Mrs. Trimpey of Baraboo, Wisconsin, who lived to be ninety three years of age. When she died she left a Will which she had written ten days before she died. The relatives tried to break it. On account of my mother, I at- tended the trial and showed them a letter written by Mrs. Trimpey four days before she died. The writing was perfect, the wording was perfect and it fully showed that she was in her right mind. That letter greatly helped to cause the will to stand.

One time at the Oliver Opera House in South Bend, there was a home talent play. An out of town man was there for twenty days in advance, teaching the actors and actresses to act in a serious show. The theatre was packed, but when the show started there were cat calls from the gallery, so the curtain came down and in ten minutes the curtain went up again. But the cat calls were worse, so the curtain came down again. The teacher of the group went out in front of the curtain, and held his hand up for quiet before speaking. It quieted down, so he spoke as follows, "You know, folks, I have traveled for twenty years from coast to coast, in many towns and cities. In many of the cities and small towns, one will find now and then an idiot. But South Bend, Indiana, has a larger percentage of them than any place I have ever been." The curtain went up for the third time and there were no more cat calls.

When A. B. Winey, who is still living, was 98 years old he called at the office. While there he told me this story, "My great-great grandfather and grandmother, with eight children, in 1790 boarded a sailing vessel in Europe, to sail for New York. It took eight weeks. They got almost to America, when a bad storm and strong wind blew the boat almost all the way back to Europe. The ocean was so rough that all of their eight children died from seasickness, not all at once, but at different times, one by one, and all were buried at sea. Their father and mother were also seasick, but they survived the very rough trip.

H. E. Bucklen, when he died in 1918, owned 28 separate properties in Elkhart. After his death, the heirs could not find any abstracts for the properties he owned. So, in selling all of these properties, they had to order new abstracts, which cost them several thousand dollars. Years later, they found all the abstracts in the attic of the Bucklen Chicago residence, hidden away in traveling valises.

John had a brick factory building on Elkhart Avenue that had 40,000 square feet of floor space, which he remodeled during a cold winter. In the center of the factory he had erected an extra large coal burning stove, on top of which he placed a 50 gallon empty steel barrel, which he had filled with water. This barrel of water heated the entire space, as the building inside was warm. Without the barrel of hot water, the building would have been much colder.

John at one time had a six room house rented to a tenant who offered $1,350.00 cash for the house and lot, which was on an alley. John agreed to sell the property for that price, so ordered the abstract brought to date. But before it was finished, the man saw a new automobile he could buy for the same amount, so he bought the car and while he was learning to drive it, he ran into a tree and completely wrecked the car. He had no insurance, so he had no car, had no house and no bank account.

The American Coating Mill Company, who owned a dam across the Elkhart River near their paper mill, were sued for eight thousand dollars by a gardner who owned twelve acres up the river. John had sold him this twelve acres three years before for six hundred dollars. John notified the management of the value of the land, so the lawsuit never came to trial as the mill attorney told the other attorney of the $600.00 sale.

One time my father and mother stopped at a hotel in Chicago and slept on an extra good mattress. They inquired from the hotel clerk where they could get such a mattress. The clerk got the information, so father and mother went to the store, picked out two twin mattresses, and found them to be very high priced. When they told the salesman to send them to Elkhart, the clerk was much surprised and remarked that one hour before another Elkhart man had also bought a mattress of the same make. When father was told who it was, he was surprised as the man was always very close with his money. When father saw him several weeks later, he said to him, "Why did you buy such a high priced mattress in Chicago?" The man promptly replied, "I figured out, John, that there is where I spend one third of my time."

About the year 1928 there was a new extra nice addition laid out on the outskirts of Indianapolis, towards the North, and the realestate man who originally owned the land sold about fifteen contracts on vacant lots to my father at a discount.

The payments were kept up on most of the contracts until about 1930, when the depression started. After the worst of the depression, a number of years later, John had eight lots in this addition left on his hands.

About 1936 he received a letter from an Indianapolis realestate man, inquiring what price he would take for a certain lot, allowing the agent 5% commission.

John sent him a list of all eight lots with a price on each lot listed and allowing the agent a 10% commission on all cash received and 5% commission on time payments. The agent wrote back and stated: "Why do you suggest 10% commission, when I offered to work for 5%?" John wrote back and stated, "He who is paid well, works well."

Within eighteen months that agent sold every lot for John and got cash for each one. His last letter stated, "I am only sorry, Mr. Fieldhouse, that you do not have any more Indianapolis property to sell." That agent worked extra well for John, because he was well paid.

One time a woman came to the office and told me that she bought a property of an Elkhart business man during the 1933 depression at a very low price, paying him a down payment, plus a monthly payment each month until paid out. She never missed a payment for three years, then fell and broke her arm, then missed payments for six months while not working. But just as she went back to work again, she received a thirty day notice to vacate the property. The owner of the contract had shown the property to another buyer the day before the notice was served. He priced it double what she was to pay for it, as then the worst of the depression was over. She came to me for help. I figured out her payments she had receipts for, showed her the balance she still owed, and told her she still had some equity in the property, in my opinion. She took my figures and showed them to the owner of her contract. He immediately stepped to his phone, called me up and said, "What business have you figuring out my contract?" I told him, "The woman asked me to figure it, as you would not figure it out for her when she asked you to." I also said, "The woman said you told her you were going to set her out." He said, "You bet I am." I said, "If you set her out I will get the abstractor to give me a list of all the real estate you own in Elkhart, and will then call on all your tenants and contracting buyers to get information. Then I will turn all information over to the Internal Revenue Department and tell them to check you up, as this woman asked you a number of times for her balance due, but you would never give it to her. On all her receipts it just states, "On account." This woman remained in the house, made her monthly payments and finally got her deed. Without my help, she would have lost her equity in the property.

In 1939 I bought eight acres of an old gravel pit within one and a half miles from the office. Christiana Creek runs through the property and I thought the property could be developed into a good swimming pool, which I made and named it "High Dive Swimming Pool." The first winter the ice was one foot thick, the pond was about three hundred by four hundred feet. I had the Elkhart Bridge & Iron Company drive eight pilings in the center of the pond where the water was thirteen feet deep. On top of these a diving platform was built, so one could dive at three, six, nine, twelve, fifteen or eighteen feet. In 1940 a place for keeping Lake Michigan sand was built and I received six railroad car loads. A forty five foot high Dutch Windmill was built, also suitable dressing rooms, caretaker's home, modern toilet rooms, an observation building and grandstand. Two dams were built across Christiana Creek so that one fifth of the creek drained through the swimming pool. I operated this pool for four years. Now I rent it to the City of Elkhart Park Department. They have operated it for nine years and are now talking about buying it. Several thousand persons flock there on a warm day. They charge no admission. I used to charge twenty five cents. Each year they have a water carnival, which is also free.

For many years Elkhart has had four moving picture theatres. The Bucklen Theatre management has lost money for the last two years. They came to me and wanted advice, as they had a lease which would run for seven more years, as it was a ten year lease. I suggested that the Boston Store, which had operated in Elkhart for forty eight years, wanted to rent a store room, as their building was badly run down and their lease was most up. Arrangements were made for them to rent the theatre. It has now been remodeled into a very beautiful store. A new level floor was laid after the seats were taken out, with a two foot drop, with seven foot wide ramp leading down. The gallery was left vacant. The suspended ceiling is not higher than twelve feet above the floor. The front of the stage at the footlights has a wall erected, so the stage can be used for storage, as the ceiling of the stage is 100 feet high. That part will not have to be heated in winter. In this way the theatre lease was solved and the store is a very beautiful one.

About thirty years ago a woman called to see father, to ask what price to charge for two lots she had bought in Los Angeles, California, about eighteen years before. She had originally paid $500.00 for the two lots as an investment. Some man had written her asking what price she would take for them. John told her to write back and ask $4,000.00 and then see what he would write back. The man wrote back that he would take the lots. He enclosed a $200.00 check and stated he would send the balance as soon as the abstract was passed on by his attorney. In two weeks she had the total of $4,000.00 additional bank account.

She then decided to take a trip to Los Angeles and see that city again. When she got there, she could not find the lots she had recently sold. She remembered a grocery building that was two blocks away from her lots, but where her lots seemed to be, there was a building on every one. So she asked the groceryman if he could help her on a puzzle. The groceryman did not catch on at first, but finally said: "Oh, I know who you are. There is a man who owned two lots on the next street and nearly two years ago he decided to build a three story six unit apartment building on his lots. He would live in one unit and rent the other five. So he built the building at a big expense, but accidently

Main Street, 1957.

built the building on the wrong lots. He built on your lots. When he found out about his mistake he wanted to get in touch with you, but did not have your address."

"He told the Collector of Taxes to get your address for him, but in the tax rush, it was overlooked. The next year he told the Tax Collector that he would give $100.00 for your address and he got it. He was very much pleased when you sent the abstract." Before that he was a sick man, as he knew you could claim the improvements if you knew about his mistake.

About the year 1904 my mother was in Chicago and picked out some nice wall paper for our parlor and sitting room, which cost $8.00 per roll, which was considered an extra high price at that period of time. When the express man brought in the small bundle of wall paper to the office the total charges were $140.00. The expressman remarked: "That is what I call extravagance." My opinion now is that it was the cheapest wall paper we ever bought, as it lasted for a period of forty years. It still looked good when we finally took it off.

One time about 1905 we had a rental house occupied but did not know it. I sent a woman to look at the house. She returned and said it was occupied. I thought she probably got the wrong house. Two days later a man went to look at the same house and he reported it was occupied. At five o'clock John went to the house to see who was in it and found there were seventeen persons counting adults and children all eating supper around the dining room table. John asked the man at the door how they all happened to move into that house. His reply was that they moved to Elkhart by a horse drawn moving van from Cassopolis, Michigan, twenty miles away. No one would rent them a house on account of such a large family. So when darkness came and the team was just about ready to quit, they saw this house was vacant and moved in. "Now, I have the rent for you, if you will give me the amount." John told him $15.00. The man pulled out a roll of bills from his pocket large enough to choke a calf and paid the rent. Several years later he bought the place and has lived there for more than 50 years. Some property owners would have told the wandering family to vacate as soon as possible.

I well remember the days when there were no automobiles on our highways. Before 1898 Elkhart had no automobiles. So I have lived during a great period of time. On account of this, during the past seventeen years, I have bought thirteen antique automobiles, which I have stored in three different places. I have also bought two old hacks, two old hearses and many other items, for a museum, which I intend to build in the near future, to remind people of the "good old days." My office has many antique items in it, and the office windows attract many passers by every day. I have a miniature Mississippi paddle wheel river boat in the window at the present time, plus one old time steam engine, coal car, freight car and caboose, which were found in the basement of an old house being torn down. Boat and train go well together, as the size of each is about the same scale.

The biggest compliment I ever received during my lifetime was from a seven year old boy. I owned three acres of ground, which was mostly low ground about twelve feet below sidewalk level, along Simonton Street and Christiana Creek. I wrote letters to seventeen riverside factories, notifying them that this ground was the nearest dump for any refuse they had and would welcome all fill.

In less than two years the entire tract was at sidewalk level, as I had a man there eight hours a day to show drivers where to dump. He kept the land leveled off with a hand shovel. Before I got him there, someone had dumped six large stumps on the ground at sidewalk level. One was an extra large stump, with roots about ten feet in height above ground. The five were each about three feet in diameter. The driver who delivered the big stumps tried to dump them in low ground, as he dumped them on the edge of the high bank. One of the smaller stumps had a tree trunk attached to it eight feet long. I went over one morning with a hired man. With two crowbars, we tried to lower the big stump, but could not move it one inch. The man with me said: "If you would saw off that five inch root resting against that tree trunk, it might fall to the lower level itself."

That afternoon I went over there alone with my truck. A little boy and girl, each about seven years old were returning home from school. They watched me with great interest, as I backed the truck against the large stump. When I sawed off the root, the big stump fell into the low ground twelve feet below. It jarred the ground when it hit the lower level. Then with the bumper of the truck, I pushed all the remaining stumps into the lower level. As I got out of the truck to inspect my work, I overheard the boy say to the girl: "That man is what people call a superman. He knows how to do things. When I grow up, I want to be a superman like him." In all my fifty five years in real estate, that seven year old boy paid me the highest compliment I had ever received.

My main reason for staying in business, is just to see what will happen next.

Fairytale cottage, where some of these stories were told.